W9-CEU-513

PRAISE FOR

Witch Queens, Voodoo Spirits, and Hoodoo Saints

"New Orleans is legendary, complex, and delicious, and I suspect few people know it better than Denise Alvarado. *Witch Queens, Voodoo Spirits, and Hoodoo Saints* is her love story to the practices in this great American city and to the diaspora that carried it with them wherever they settled. This is as good as the best gumbo."

—H. BYRON BALLARD, author of
Seasons of a Magical Life

"Reading Denise Alvarado's words is like sitting in the kitchen the morning before Mardi Gras, nibbling on warm pralines after devouring a heaping bowl of boiled shrimp and crawfish. As the Skull and Bone Gang rattle the iron wrought fence bearing remnants of Akan artistry, each twist and curvature of Denise's words seasons the poignantly satisfying and deliciously clever gumbo—a feast for the liberated African soul. Alvarado blends New Orleans's indigenous queens, spirits, and saints into a holy trinity that is part myth, part tall tale, and part historical accuracy, as only a daughter of the Crescent City could. Alvarado stirs each story with warmth, compassion, and salvation, while never once scorching the roux. This book is a must-have for any serious lover, devotee, or student of New Orleans from an African-centered perspective."

—MAWIYAH KAI EL-JAMAH BOMANI, award winning playwright,
author of *Spring Chickens*

"Denise Alvarado's *Witch Queens, Voodoo Spirits, and Hoodoo Saints* is the book I wish I could have read as my introduction to the folklore of New Orleans. As my surname suggests, my family has a long history in New Orleans, and I have visited many times, over more than fifty years, since

I was a small child. Despite a thorough grounding in the spiritual history of New Orleans, I learned a lot from this book. A superb account of the important spiritual figures, unusual saints, and renowned practitioners of New Orleans—a multicultural crossroads with a fascinating religious history—this book gives readers a well-rounded picture of the cross-cultural spiritual "gumbo" of New Orleans, America's most interesting city."

—CAROLINE KENNER, founder of
The Fool's Dog Tarot app

"*Witch Queens, Voodoo Spirits, and Hoodoo Saints* is filled with fascinating and lesser-known historical facts alongside insightful, detailed, and intimate introductions to the spectral or unseen—but felt!—New Orleans hidden just beneath the city's surface. Denise Alvarado brings to life the powerful divine *loa* from Africa, as well as ancestral spirits, such as Mamzelle Marie Laveau, who are the wisdom, truth, and power of its Voodoo, Hoodoo, and witchcraft practices and lore, the delicious cultural synergy or gumbo that is magical New Orleans."

—ORION FOXWOOD, author of
Mountain Conjure and Southern Rootwork

WITCH QUEENS,
VOODOO SPIRITS
& HOODOO SAINTS

A Guide to Magical New Orleans

DENISE ALVARADO

NEW HANOVER COUNTY
PUBLIC LIBRARY
201 CHESTNUT STREET
WILMINGTON, NC 28401

WEISER
BOOKS

This edition first published in 2022 by Weiser Books, an imprint of
Red Wheel/Weiser, LLC
With offices at:
65 Parker Street, Suite 7
Newburyport, MA 01950
www.redwheelweiser.com

Copyright © 2022 by Denise Alvarado
All rights reserved. No part of this publication may be reproduced or transmitted in any form or
by any means, electronic or mechanical, including photocopying, recording, or by any information
storage and retrieval system, without permission in writing from Red Wheel/Weiser, LLC.
Reviewers may quote brief passages.

ISBN: 978-1-57863-674-7
Library of Congress Cataloging-in-Publication Data available upon request.

Cover and Interior design by Kathryn Sky-Peck
Cover art © Karol Bak

Typeset in ITC Berkeley Oldstyle

Printed in the United States of America
IBI
10 9 8 7 6 5 4 3 2 1

This book contains advice and information for using herbs, spellcraft, ritual observances, shamanism,
and ritual possession and is not meant to diagnose, treat, or prescribe. It should be used to supple-
ment, not replace, the advice of your physician or other trained healthcare practitioner. If you know
or suspect you have a medical condition, are experiencing physical symptoms, or if you feel unwell,
seek your physician's advice before embarking on any medical program or treatment. Readers are
cautioned to follow instructions carefully and accurately for the best effect. Readers using the information in this book do so entirely at their own risk, and the author and publisher accept no liability
if adverse effects are caused.

To Zephyr, the Italian Greyhound,

My conjure dawg and pandemic partner,

You are my heart and my muse.

May you rest in power and joy,

Meet me at the crossroads,

Let's rise together

with the

Sun.

From all, to all, with all,

For all, through all, be all,

We thank the Ancestors and the gods of creation.

We thank the orishas, loas, and saints.

We thank the spirits; we thank Mother Earth.

We pay homage to the Mother and Father of New Orleans Voudou,

Marie Laveau and Doctor John Montenée.

We thank them for their protection, their guidance, and their
sustenance,

For showing us and allowing us to know and enjoy life to
its fullest.

Ashe!

Contents

Introduction

We desire to bequeath two things to our children; the first one is roots,
the other one is wings.

—Sudanese proverb

Charming. Soulful. Captivating. A foodies' paradise. A ghost hunter's wet dream. A veritable smorgasbord of cultures. A city that never sleeps. These words and phrases describe much of what can be seen and experienced in New Orleans. As anyone who has been to the Crescent City will tell you, you get a feeling when you are there that screams "elusive and mysterious." It's a gut-level feeling—you know there is more to it, but you just can't put your finger on it. All you know is that you want to see more, know more, and, ultimately, feel more—more of that good ole N'awlins supernatural vibe.

And New Orleans doesn't disappoint in that regard. She is inhabited by fascinating visible and invisible worlds, full of mysteries and haunted by spirits. Some legends can be connected to documented, factual people and events, while others are relegated to folklore. In this guide to supernatural New Orleans, I introduce twenty magickal figures found in Louisiana— the witch queens, Voudou spirits, and hoodoo saints—who reside in the spiritual underbelly there.

Take Mary Oneida Toups, for example, who was popular in the 1970s as the Witch Queen of New Orleans. Originally from Mississippi, Oneida founded the Religious Order of Witchcraft, the first church of witchcraft to be recognized in Louisiana. A one-line reference was made to her in the American television series *American Horror Story: Coven*, about rituals she performed at Popp's Fountain in New Orleans. This prompted a renewed interest in her among modern-day witches. Sadly, other than a few articles in the newspapers in the 1970s and one article published in *Hoodoo and Conjure Quarterly*, nothing substantial has been written about this fascinating contemporary witch. I believe I have provided the most thorough public accounting of her magick to date.

And who hasn't heard of the legendary Julia Brown, who said she would take the whole town with her when she died, and who literally did just that? Well, if you have never heard of her, you are about to meet the woman who not only owned the whole town of Frenier, she served as a healer and spiritual advisor, as well. But when the townspeople shunned her and the people began abusing the environment, the unthinkable happened.

One folk heroine I am thrilled to introduce to the world is Annie Christmas. To hear most people speak of her, she is a sort of female version of John Henry. A black version and a white version of her exists, depending on who is telling her story. But did you know she is actually a spirit in the pantheon of New Orleans Voudou?[1] She is revered as an ancestral cultural hero and has been part of local African American folklore for years. And among old-time Voudouists, there are mysteries about her that have remained hidden, only accessible to those practitioners old enough

---

1 The spelling "Voudou" is used throughout the manuscript to maintain consistency with the majority of the 19th-century sources used in my research. The spelling is also used to distinguish it from Haitian Vodou, African Vodun, and tourist voodoo.

to know of her. Here, her story is shared from the perspectives of legend, lore, and Voudou.

Indeed, it is impossible to write about the mysteries of magickal New Orleans without discussing Voudou, which arrived in New Orleans with the first Africans brought as chattels in the early 1700s. With the enslaved came their beliefs in traditional African cosmologies, which were in stark contrast to Christianity in some, yet not all, ways.

Upon the implementation of the Louisiana Black Codes, everyone was forcibly baptized into the Catholic faith. As the newly converted slaves became familiar with the mystical rites and saints of Catholicism, they discovered similarities to their own religions. They used that knowledge to cloak their religious beliefs and deities behind the veil of Catholicism. Some Catholic saints were associated with Voudou spirits by function and others by resemblance, a dynamic known as syncretization.

For example, Baron Samedi became syncretized with St. Expedite, as they are both associated with the Dead. Papa Legba, who, in his native Dahomey, guards the crossroads and entrances to temples, homes, and compounds, became widely served in Haiti and New Orleans for opening roads and clearing away obstacles. Legba holds the keys to the Spirit World like St. Peter, who holds the keys to heaven's gates. Eventually, many Catholic saints were adopted into Voudou as ancestor spirits, with their own identities separate from the Voudou spirits.

Some of the Voudou spirits I feature here survived in the underground New Orleans Voudou scene as part of the same resistance that began in the mid-1700s in Louisiana. Jean San Malo, aka St. Maroon, was an actual person who gained infamy as a runaway slave who mocked justice. His audacity made him famous. In reality, his story is a testament to his cunning, resourcefulness, intelligence, and leadership. Scarcely touched upon in the popular magickal literature, he is as relevant today as in the 1700s. Here, I provide an account of his life as a political resistor and New Orleans Voudou saint. This perspective enhances the most common narrative of him as a runaway slave who helped other slaves escape to safety in the swamps surrounding New Orleans.

An intriguing characteristic of New Orleans's magickal traditions is found in cultural Catholicism. This includes the saints—both the canonized and folk variety—who are celebrated and observed within the Catholic religion and among Voudouists, conjure workers, Spiritualists, and hoodoos. I would imagine that folks unfamiliar with the spiritual traditions of New Orleans might find the revelation alarming. Staunch Catholics may consider it sacrilege. Nevertheless, there are full-blown magickal practices associated with the traditions of these saints, in addition to the Catholic Church's usual mystical rites. In fact, there is a whole side to New Orleans's popular saints and sacramentals that is only seen through the lens of the Catholic Voudou. In this book, I provide a window into that world.

In addition to witch queens and Voudou spirits, I cover several of the various New Orleans hoodoo saints referenced by folklorist Harry Middleton Hyatt in his seminal work *Hoodoo-Conjuration-Witchcraft-Rootwork*. These saints are the stars of the little-known Catholic Conjure tradition. They are widely accepted as holy saints of devotion for Catholics in general and are enmeshed in local celebrations such as Mardi Gras and St. Joseph's Day. Here, I present the untold magickal lore of a number of these beloved saints: St. Anthony, St. Roch, St. Joseph, St. Peter, and the most curious saint of all, St. Expedite.

• • •

As mysterious as the city of New Orleans is, it is the stories of the people, spirits, and saints that make it so magickal. *Witch Queens, Voodoo Spirits, and Hoodoo Saints* is a book of these untold, sacred stories. I am honored to share some of the mysteries that make up the cultural history of the city in which I was born and raised. In doing so, I hope to inform and entertain. At the same time, I hope to make New Orleans's magickal and spiritual practices less scary and more familiar to the average person. Our mysteries are not what the movies portray, though some kernels of truth may be found there. Hopefully, you will discover that we have more in common than not. And our differences? May they be perceived not in fear but with awe and wonderment.

—DENISE ALVARADO

All Hallow's Eve in the year of the Pandemic, 2020, during Mercury Retrograde

Annie Christmas. Mixed media by Denise Alvarado, 2014

1

Annie Christmas, Daughter of the Mississippi River

You got a bully on these few blasted acres of mud you call a town? Get him out of his hole if he'll come out! I'll tear the hide off him and hang it up to dry in the morning sun. I'm a cross between a snapping turtle and a swamp gator. I was weaned on panther's milk, and I eat grizzly bear claws for breakfast. Send your white liver champion down the river landing. I'll turn his bones into goofer dust. This is Annie Christmas! Y'all hear me?!

—ANNIE CHRISTMAS

She emits foreboding energy to those standing in her presence who have done wrong and a feeling of safety and security to those she has come to assist. She's a daughter of the Mississippi Delta, born in the city of New Orleans, stronger than any man and a hero to every woman.

Annie Christmas was the original superhero before superheroes were a thing. Her stories inspired both enslaved and free African Americans in pre–Civil War Louisiana. Her reputation preceded her along the Mississippi River Valley as a force to be reckoned with. In fact, she had the reputation of being an annihilator of bullies. Just let her see a man pick on someone, and once she was done with him, he never acted that way again. She even scared off big ole Mike Fink from the docks of the lower Mississippi.

Even more than a defender of the underdog, Annie was ahead of her time. She insisted on equality in vocation and treatment between genders. She took on occupations typically reserved for men. She resisted the social mores of the times, like the usual plaçage arrangements popular during the early 19th century in New Orleans, whereby white men arranged common-law households with non-European women of African, Native American, and Creole descent. There were numerous economic benefits from such arrangements, including freedom for enslaved family members. Even so, Annie Christmas rejected such an arrangement, viewing it as a male-dominated, racist social institution. Instead, she ran away to the frontier of the Mississippi River to become a well-respected keelboatman.

Scant information about Annie Christmas is available in the written record. One description about her comes from a local informant from New Orleans named Eddie Simms, who was interviewed by the Federal Writers' Project (FWP) in the 1930s. Simms was a fifty-four-year-old longshoreman who had worked on the riverfront for some twenty-odd years. He remembered Annie Christmas as a "pie lady and bucket woman who used to bring lunch to the longshoremen on de riverfront." He confirmed Annie was a black woman who had many sons who also worked on the riverfront.

"She was a bad woman," stated Simms, "who used to fight wid men, especially if dey didn't pay her her money." And when asked what he remembered about Annie Christmas in particular, he confirmed that she could outdrink anyone on the riverfront, downing a barrel of beer and ten quarts of whiskey without stopping. "Sometimes she would git in fights around de whiskey joints and whip everybody she saw" (Dillon, Folder 575, 23).

As a folk heroine, Annie Christmas has been treated as racially fluid in the South. You could say she was gender fluid, as well. Depending on who you talk to, she could be black, a former slave, or white with a "small but carefully trimmed mustache" (Asbury 1936, 82). Simms, however, said that he didn't know how anyone could say she was white when, at the time, "dere certainly was no white women on de riverfront" (Dillon, Folder 575, 20). Either way, black or white, all agree she could outwork a plantation mule.

In the context of New Orleans Voudou, Annie Christmas is of African descent. At some point, she was adopted into New Orleans Voudou's pantheon of spirits. Don't ask me when; I haven't a clue. That fact remains a magickal mystery. But suffice it to say, it was a long time ago.

Like the Catholic saints, each spirit in the New Orleans Voudou pantheon has its own unique characteristics. They have special symbols, days of the week, feast days, and life domains over which they exert influence. When an individual is experiencing problems in a given area, they will call on the spirit or saint that governs that sphere of influence for assistance. To that end, Annie is petitioned for protection and defense, removing obstacles, empowering women, and destroying bullies.

Whether discussing Annie Christmas in the context of folklore or folk religion, trying to discover Annie's origins leads mostly to oral history and archetype instead of any historical person. Of course, that doesn't mean she is purely fictional; her origin story is full of mysteries, as you will soon learn.

ANNIE'S ORIGINS

Where did Annie come from? Where? From the yonder seas out there. From the mountains of the moon, the far-off land of the Cameroon. Damballah's Child it has been said, others say a King's instead. Greatest of the Nubian greats with bloodlines back beyond recorded date. . . . Others claim a mortal birth, a god and goddess straight on earth. (Conrad 1956)

Some folks say Annie Christmas is simply the fictional star of a tall tale or legend. Some say she is a Voudou ancestral spirit based on an actual person. Indeed, there are many different stories about Annie's origins and exploits—including those versions with adult themes. Most of them center on her activities along the Mississippi River.

One version of her life describes her as a huge, coal-black negress with twelve coal-black sons, each seven feet tall. In another version, she was a river tramp, the wife of a keelboatman, possessed of enormous strength. One tale had her shot to death in a brawl in a New Orleans gambling house. In Negro legend, she committed suicide for love; her body was placed aboard a coal-black barge by her twelve coal-black sons, and all of them floated down the Mississippi to the sea, never to be seen again. (Haskin 1961, 88)

The most commonly told origin story promotes Annie as the subject of a hoax perpetrated by two white writers in New Orleans. According to Mary Rose Bradford, in the 1920s, Lyle Saxon and Mary's husband, Roark Bradford, were having drinks in the French Quarter when they fabricated the tale of Annie Christmas as a joke. Roark Bradford was a well-known writer who lived in New Orleans and was the editor for the *Times-Picayune* newspaper. Lyle Saxon was also a renowned writer and reporter for the *Times-Picayune*. Apparently, the two men were known for perpetrating hoaxes upon innocents for their personal amusement, especially after getting a few drinks under their belts.

It seems that they were running out of material about New Orleans's folk characters, so they decided to make up a female version of John Henry or Paul Bunyan. Saxon would "discover" some ancient manuscripts about a mythical Annie while he and Bradford made up a bunch of stories about a woman who lived on the river and had superpowers and "flaming red hair and a temper to match" (Kolb 2013, 134). They would call her Mary Christmas, but Mary Rose said her husband didn't think anyone would believe that. So they settled on the name Annie Christmas. The result? Folklore (Thomas 2011, 32).

Saxon and Bradford supposedly took their well-fabricated story and published it in the *Times-Picayune*. I have searched high and low for any articles published about a black or white Annie Christmas in the 1920s, and thus far, the only thing that came up was a review for one of Saxon's books in which he wrote this about her:

> Annie was a river tramp, the wife of a keelboatman, and was said to possess enormous strength. Sometimes "Annie" is described as keeping a sort of floating saloon aboard a flatboat. At other times she is pictured as disguising herself as a man. In such costume, she fought, gambled, and made love to women who did not penetrate her disguise. (Saxon 1927, 138)

Some years after Saxon's book came out, Carl Carmer collected tall tales for his book, *The Hurricane's Children*. He approached Saxon and Bradford for information. They reportedly told him all about Annie Christmas. As a result of their conversations, Carmer included Annie's story in his book in 1937.

While white writers may have made up a white, red-headed Annie Christmas, stories about a black Annie Christmas have been around for years. Indeed, if Annie Christmas is the result of a hoax perpetrated by Saxon and Bradford in the 1920s, the evidence is not definitive. We have Mary Rose's account, but I have yet to see the article they supposedly printed in the *Times-Picayune* during their specified time frame. Of course, it could be that the reason for not finding the elusive piece is because neither actually wrote a word about her for the newspapers. According to John Thompson, a writer for the *Tennessean*,

> Considering their inventive genius and talent for exploiting tall stories, it seems rather a shame that neither ever wrote a line about Annie Christmas. They merely dreamed her up for the amazement of Carl Carmer . . . By way of a joke, they began to tell him about Annie Christmas, making her up as they went along. (Thompson 1948, 74)

In my quest to uncover Annie's origins, I searched for articles in the 1800s that mentioned anyone named Annie Christmas, a flatboat, and drowning. I figured that if I could find evidence of an Annie Christmas associated with the Mississippi River, keelboats, cotton, or any of the key parts of her legend, we could possibly connect her with an actual historical figure or event.

To that end, I found mention of an Annie Christman from Jamaica, Queens, who attempted suicide by jumping off a ferryboat in 1896. It was mentioned in the *New York Times* (1896, 8) as:

> The case of Mrs. Annie Christman of Jamaica, who jumped into the East River from a ferryboat Tuesday night to drown herself, was before Justice Ingram, in Long Island City, yesterday. Her examination was postponed until tomorrow.

The year of the alleged attempted suicide is likely too late in the century to make this Annie Christman the Annie Christmas of folklore. But, then again, we don't have any firm dates of her birth—or anything else, for that matter. It is quite possible that this Annie Christman story was absorbed into her legend. According to lore, she commits suicide by jumping into the river off a keelboat or riverboat after being rejected by her lover. The parallels between the two stories are hard to discount completely.

Whether or not we ever definitively determine the origins of Annie Christmas, she has found a permanent place in the legends of old New Orleans. She appears in books, plays, folklore, and Voudou as a spirit in its pantheon. "She is the real thing," writes Thompson. "Her legend will continue to grow just as lustily as if she had been born among the anonymous frontier spinners of folk yarns." (Thompson 1948, 74)

FOLKLORE HEROINE

Annie Christmas worked the docks along the Mississippi River as a three-barrel flatbed unloader just like the menfolk did. She could walk a gangplank with a barrel of flour under each arm and one on her head to boot. Once, an obnoxious longshoreman was running his mouth, taking too long to load the keelboat. Having no time for such foolishness, Annie slapped him across the face and loaded up the keelboat herself. Then, in a fit of impatience, she towed that keelboat all the way from New Orleans to Natchez without losing her breath. Her tow was so fast and smooth that the boat hydroplaned over the water; this feat was the origin of the saying in the river towns: "As strong as Annie Christmas."

Poling a keelboat is a job that requires a tremendous amount of strength. Boats typically carry heavy supplies such as bales of cotton, lumber, flour, and people. But Annie Christmas was a woman with superhuman power. She was reportedly six feet eight inches tall—heck, some say she was a whopping seven feet tall—and weighed 250 pounds, maybe more. During the day, she dressed in men's clothing. And she always wore her pearl necklace, whether she wore trousers or a fancy dress. Defying the norms of a male-dominated workplace and society, Annie purchased a boat of her own and became a well-respected keelboat captain in her own right.

Now, Annie was larger than life in many ways, but there were three things she just couldn't stand: weakmindedness, laziness, and bullies (Conrad 1956). She had no tolerance for intolerance and could get mad as a hornet when confronted by mischief. Her no-nonsense approach to dealing with people was punctuated by the red turkey feather she wore in her hat that signified her status as a champion fighter.

Take the time Mike Fink came to town, for instance. As usual, Annie was hard at work carrying a bale of cotton and getting ready to load it onto the boat. Fink had never seen a woman working the docks before; Annie's imposing size didn't seem to impress him, either. He was bigger than life himself, and although he may have been really strong, he sure wasn't very smart.

"Why aren't you home cooking dinner and keeping house instead of doing men's work, woman?" Mike laughingly hurled his patronizing comment at Annie.

Suddenly, silence came over the docks. You could hear a pin drop. Everyone was watching because things were about to get real.

Annie was in a kneeling position, just about to pick up another bale of cotton. She cocked her head from side to side. Snap. Crackle. Pop. She stood up, looked Mike Fink dead in the eye, and with a calm voice, stated, "Mister, you seem to think you have an opinion that matters here." Then, she lifted that 480-pound bale of cotton over her head, causing the collective gasps of everyone watching. She threw that bale of cotton clear over Mike Fink's head, slamming it into the water with such force it caused a ten-foot tidal wave that carried him 150 miles away to Natchez. And then, as if nothing had happened, Annie returned to her work. And Mike Fink? Well, he hasn't been seen in New Orleans ever since (Miller 2013).

All roughhousing aside, Annie loved a good time. She loved parties, gambling, drinking, and raising a general ruckus on Bourbon Street. And she could drink any man under the table:

> She would put down a barrel of beer and chase it with ten quarts of whiskey without stopping. Men used to buy her whiskey just to see her drink. Sometimes she got mad in a barroom, beat up every man in the place, and wrecked the joint. Sometimes she did it for fun. (Saxon 1945, 376)

Annie wasn't always in fighting mode, though. She was known to go to Congo Square and join the Voudous in their dances and ceremonial activities. They say she was gifted with the far eye—she saw spirits, foretold the future, and had second sight. She danced the bamboula, always came with a pocket full of money, and gave it all to the poor. They say she danced with the devil, but that's not true. There is no devil in Voudou.

That said, Annie was sensitive to energy, and she could sense evil and maleficence. She was known to stare down vile spirits and win. She wasn't afraid of looking evil in the eye, whether it manifested in people or in spirit form.

In the evenings, Annie liked to go out on the town with her girlfriends. Some evenings, she wore a red silk dress with her hair in an updo into which she would stick peacock feathers. Like the celebrated Voudou Queen of New Orleans, Marie Laveau, Annie could get away with not wearing the law-enforced tignon required by all women of color at the time. If she did wear one, it was because she wanted to and not because some racist society told her she had to.

ANNIE GETS HER NAME

Folklore suggests that Annie got her name when she arrived in New Orleans on Christmas Day, sometime around 1800. Twelve men, eight feet tall—presumably, her sons—manned her boat. She landed on the riverbanks and stunned witnesses with her presence. She was described as extraordinarily dark and tall, resembling a circus giant. She was amazing, they thought, like a female Sampson or Hercules, a Nubian Queen, definitely majestic. Grace Jones comes to mind. Pull up to my keelboat baby . . .

As she stood on the riverbank with her twelve coal-black sons standing behind her, Annie attracted one misguided man who intended to capture and enslave her. "You're mine by the right of my rawhide whip!" he exclaimed. The other men standing by him began to approach her.

Annie proclaimed, "You two blooded swine! You are swine whose sin is the worst of mankind!" The would-be slaver then threatened to tame her mouth by flogging her. He raised his arm, whip in hand, and faster than a hare, she grabbed that whip in mid-air. Annie threw the would-be slaver to the ground, stomped on his ribs, tore off his ear, and rolled him in the Mississippi mud. She whooped that would-be slaver's ass so bad, she slung him into the sky straight into another county, where he was "worth no more now than a dead skunk's bounty." She showed them all, then and there, who she was and what she was about, and it wasn't about being anybody's slave.

Well, the astounded crowd followed Annie throughout the town and proclaimed to all who would listen that she was Annie Christmas, a champion of God's forgotten children. "This day will be remembered for a long time to come! She walks in glory with the saints!" And then she vanished at the Natchez Trace, a sudden legend of her ancient race (Conrad 1956).

According to this legend, her name is honored on St. John's Eve by the pope of Voudou, Marie Laveau, whose congregation embraced her as the black goddess of the Motherland. Like Marie Laveau, Annie had a reputation for nursing the sick, helping the poor, and standing up for the underdog. The years brought Annie far wider fame; poor folk of all races blessed her name. She mothered the weak and fought the evil strong, but when it came to love, her luck ran wrong.

ANNIE GETS HER MAN

Annie's first love in the new land was a gambling man called Goldmouth Bill from Natchez, Under-the-Hill. He was a real player. He liked cards—a lot. But he was a bottom dealer. One day he was accused of cheating in a card game. According to legend, they actually cut his head off for cheating! When Annie found out, she was so distraught, her wailing blew down a hundred oak trees.

Annie's next great love was the infamous pirate known as Jean Lafitte. He was notorious for doing piratety things, like smuggling and thieving. They say she ran off with him and his band of pirates one evening after dancing with the Voudous on Congo Square. She supposedly followed him into the Battle of New Orleans. She loved that bad boy. He was hung. But Lafitte's days were numbered. "I love you, Annie Christmas," were the last words he uttered as they placed the rope around his neck to hang him. Annie drowned her tears in sorrow, cursed the past, present, and tomorrow. She wallowed in a sea of fiery rum, crying, "That's all the love for me 'til kingdom come."

After a spell, Annie married Charlie, another gambling man with whom she had her twelve sons. "Good people, I'm the most renowned, prolific Mother on the Earth. I bore twelve sons in a single birth!" she exclaimed. Her twelve coal-black sons were all born at the same time. She had plenty of other babies, too, but these were her favorites. They say whenever she got ready to have a baby, she drank a quart of whiskey and lay down somewhere. Afterward, she had another quart and went straight back to work.

ANNIE GETS HER GRIS GRIS

Well, poor Annie Christmas, so unlucky in love. In another part of her legend, the losses she experienced were too much to bear, so she gave up on ever finding a lasting mate. Then, she turned to Voudou to deal with her unfortunate fate.

"I'll buy a powerful gris gris," she said, to deal with being alone. "Love's not for me, what's two is three. This Voudou charm my heart sets fancy free" (Conrad 1956).

A gris gris is considered a hallmark of powerful New Orleans Voudou magick. Most people buy a gris gris charm to bring love to themselves, but not Annie Christmas. She resigned herself to living out her life alone. And she wanted to be happy, so she bought that gris gris for love—self-love.

In all likelihood, she probably got that gris gris from Marie Laveau, the Voudou Queen of New Orleans, during the 1800s. They say that Annie was a frequent attendee at the Laveau rituals. No doubt the gris gris would have contained things like Balm of Gilead for emotional comfort, red rose petals for love, lotus root for spiritual protection, rosemary for a woman's worth, a High John root for all-round success, and a fixed acorn[2] for good luck in gambling. She may have been resigned to living alone, but she still planned on having a good time! Marie Laveau would have blessed that bag three times in the name of the Father, the Son, and the Holy Spirit.

---

2   An object that is fixed in the context of Voudou folk magick and hoodoo is one that has been ritually prepared for a specific purpose. In this case, a fixed acorn refers to an acorn that has been ritually prepared to bring good luck and abundant winnings.

Then, she would have called down the sacred serpent Li Grand Zombi into the gris gris bag before handing it over to Annie. Ashé! Ashé! Ashé!

After Annie got her gris gris, she came to terms with her self-professed fate. They say she grew a mustache, cut her hair, and started dressing like a man. That's when she got the job as a three-barrel flatboat unloader. Later, she became captain of her own keelboat. She was happy with her life like this for a long time.

ANNIE'S NECKLACE

A symbol of Annie's power was her necklace, made of pearls or beads, and it was said to be a record of all her heroic deeds. They say she wore that necklace everywhere—at work, night, and play—as a constant reminder of all the men she'd slay. Some say she wore it every day whether she was dressed as a man or a woman, working on the docks, towing a keelboat, or Ballin' the Jack at a juke joint. Another version says it's a necklace made of yellow beads. Yet another story says it was made of alligator teeth. Still another, more macabre version, says her necklace was made up of the eyes, noses, and ears she collected during her beat-down activities. Gross. I like the pearls version, personally.

When she died, they say her necklace was thirty feet long—a proper memento. It could have been longer; only some of the fights were so easy Annie didn't feel it was honorable to commemorate them. They say she only recorded the white men she defeated because if she had also recorded black men, her necklace would have been way too long. Or she would have run out of pearls.

THE FLOATING BORDELLO

One of the enduring legends about Annie Christmas is that she owned and operated a floating brothel of scarlet women. During this time of her life, "she donned skirts, shaved her mustache, and became the captain of a floating bordello, catering to the emotional needs of lusty river men," writes Herbert Asbury in his book, *The French Quarter.* She provided a coveted service to longshoremen, river pirates, keelboatmen, and stevedores. She was known to stage fights and have contests, and, of course, because no one could beat her, Annie always won first prize. She also offered up a keg of whiskey and loads of cash to the woman who could entertain the most men in a given period. Needless to say, the prize was always won by Annie (Asbury 1936, 82).

Well, whenever Annie got in the mood, she would dress up in her finest and invite her girlfriends to join her for a ride up the Mississippi River. They would stop at all the river towns along the way. Annie would tow that keelboat up to the river's edge at each town where a man waited for one of the ladies. One by one, they would disembark the boat until finally, the last girlfriend would get off and join the gentleman waiting for her on the shore. Annie would be left standing alone.

It was okay; Annie never needed a man herself, though she thoroughly enjoyed the men she did have. Some say she was a Madame—she never put herself out for money but collected a portion of what her girlfriends made. She was good with this arrangement.

Once, she was relaxing on her boat in Natchez, waiting for her girlfriends to return from their dates, when she saw a fancy paddle-wheel-steamboat floating by. She heard lots of laughter and music. So, she decided to get on board that fancy steamboat and join the party.

Lucky for Annie, it was a grand affair! She had a wonderful time doing her three favorite things: eating, drinking, and gambling. Throw in a bit of arm wrestling with the guys, and the night was going perfectly.

Suddenly, however, the tides turned. Coal-black thunderclouds rolled in, followed by torrential rain. The winds blew hard, and the fancy steamboat shook as the rain poured down without mercy. That steamboat was swaying to and fro, and the people began to panic.

Annie approached the captain. She watched as he began to steer the steamboat through a narrow channel that was going to land them on a sandbar. "Don't go that way, you'll get us stuck in a sandbar for sure!" Annie exclaimed.

"Woman, mind your business! This is my boat! I'm the captain here!" he shouted back over the roaring winds and thunderclaps.

Annie only pleaded with him for so long. She knew they were on borrowed time as it was, and this captain was too proud to listen.

So, Annie managed to convince everyone on the boat to get on her keelboat and let her pole them to safety. And everyone did just that. Everyone, that is, except the captain. He ended up disappearing that night into the storm, along with his fancy paddle-wheel steamboat.

Annie got her keelboat back to New Orleans from Natchez in such a hurry that it amazed everyone. And she wasn't even out of breath! She was fully enshrined as a hero that day and was lauded all along the Mississippi for her heroic deeds.

ANNIE'S DEATH

All legends have their variations, largely dependent upon the person who is telling the story. We each like to add our own embellishments and emphasize our favorite versions of events. There are several versions of Annie's death that I am aware of, and they each describe different ways in which she died.

One version emphasizes Annie's badassery and how she never met a man she couldn't lick. Putting the beat-down on bullies was a fun pastime for her. And everyone knew she could take on ten men with one arm tied behind her back, so any sane person knew not to act a fool in her presence. Nevertheless, one day she met her match. She was so impressed by this guy that she fell madly in love. She dressed in all her finery. She poured on the charm. But it didn't work. The man was not interested in a romantic relationship with her. Annie took the rejection awfully hard. She became sullen and depressed. They say she put on her red satin dress and put three of her most beautiful peacock feathers in her hair. She spritzed herself with Follow Me Boy perfume like she was going out on the town. Then, she wrapped that thirty-foot pearl necklace around her neck and hung herself.

But another legend recounts the story differently. Remember when Annie married the gambling man named Charlie, with whom she had her twelve coal-black sons? The smallest son was seven feet tall before the age of six years old!

Well, one day, Charlie went to a gambling house and put his money on red at roulette. The operator spun the wheel, and the little ball bounced until it landed on red! Charlie didn't bat an eye, and again he placed his money on red. And again, fortune was with him. Well, Charlie kept playing that wheel until he amassed a hefty $16,000! That was a whole ton of money back in Annie's day.

Everyone kept telling Charlie he needed to stop, but Charlie kept his eye on the wheel and didn't say a word.

Well, the banker knew he couldn't keep on going, so he had to close down the game. Still, no word from Charlie. He just sat there, staring at the wheel.

Finding no response highly unusual at this point, they took a closer look at Charlie. Deader. Than. A. Door. Nail.

I can't tell you how he died or exactly when he died, but it seems he had a heart attack at some point during all that gaming, and no one even noticed! "A dead man had broken the bank" (Swetnam 1968, 135).

Suddenly, Annie found herself a widow and $16,000 richer!

Annie would spend that money and have the fanciest funeral ever for Charlie. But first, she called her twelve sons and had a talkin' to. Then, she put on a beautiful black satin dress, put on her thirty-foot-long necklace, fixed her hair and her face, and shot herself dead.

They say the funeral was very extravagant. Per Annie's instructions, she was placed in a coal-black coffin along with her husband, Charlie. The casket was put into a coal-black hearse. They were driven by sixteen coal-black horses down to the riverfront. On each side of the hearse marched six of her coal-black sons, dressed in coal-black suits. At the riverfront, the coal-black coffin was placed on a coal-black barge. That coal-black night, with no moon shining, six sons standing on either side of her coffin cut the ropes and floated down the Mississippi River with their dead mother. The sounds of their singing voices faded as they floated farther and farther away until all that was seen was the coal-black night. They were never seen or heard from again.

Suicide is such a tragic ending to a life full of meaning and purpose. And it seems so out of character for a strong woman like Annie Christmas. Then again, all human beings are fallible. Greatness often involves tragedy. And when all of her story is considered, it seems as though love was Annie's Achilles' heel. She could not find it and keep it. Oh, she had plenty of fun with her boy toys. Still, she wanted to experience true love and a committed relationship. Sadly, it was always just out of reach.

Until she met Brimstone Pete, that is.

ANNIE GETS HER PETER

And so the story goes that Annie eventually quit the riverboat life and bought herself a tiny home near a bayou off the Natchez Trace. She bought some cows and some pigs, opted for a quiet life, and settled down. Annie finally had the peace and comfort of the home she always wanted. She was satisfied—almost.

"This single bliss is a bitter kiss," said Annie, who had begun longing for the companionship of a goodly man. She was about done with the single life, so she threw her gris gris up in the air, and it landed who knows where. Annie rested well that fateful night because she saw her love with her second sight. When she released that gris gris, so were her intentions, and before you know it, Peter Peppercorn, aka Brimstone Pete, was at her door a-knockin'.

Brimstone Pete was a trapper man and a preacher man. They say he was six feet wide and five-foot-three inches tall, nearly half Annie's size. Pete prayed his prayers, and, like Annie, he fought swamp creatures and mountain bears. He had one blue eye and one brown eye and traveled the countryside with his humble, faithful mule, preaching the Good Word and being a good man. Pete believed his mule was like the one that carried Mama Mary with Jesus in her belly to the holy city of Bethlehem.

"I'm a man of few words," he told Annie. "Will you be my wife?" Realizing the power of letting go of that gris gris, Annie said yes. And so, Pete married himself to Annie with his loyal mule standing in as a witness. In perfect harmony, a bird choir sang "amen." Her love and kisses, beans and rice, transported Pete into paradise.

Their honeymoon was relaxing in Annie's humble home, where they could sip on sweet tea, laugh, and watch the alligators roam. They told stories of the reptilian swamp gods, Uncle Monday and Papa Gator, and a particularly foul creature known as Gator Nick. They shared their favorite story from the Old Testament about that Israelite named Jonah. Jonah had been called by God to be a prophet but refused his divine mission and, instead, left on a sea voyage.

Yes, Brimstone Pete was a preacher man, but he didn't get to preach with Annie. She appreciated a fine Christian man and enjoyed Bible stories, but Damballah Wedo was the God she knew. So, Brimstone Pete hitched up his mule and bid Annie adieu, and he set out to preach while the moon was still new.

Pete was to return within three weeks. While he was gone, Annie busied herself with tasks around her home. She went to Congo Square and left food offerings of red beans and Creole rice for the hungry there, as was customary among the Voudous. But Annie stayed out of the gambling houses. She refrained from getting involved in the riverfront shenanigans of her not-so-distant past.

Six weeks went by, and Annie wept as she wondered what had become of her true love, the man who had manifested when she released her attachment to that powerful love gris gris. She knew Peter was a man of his word and that he would return because he said he would. But he was nowhere in sight. The folks in town hadn't seen him either.

Suddenly, a morbid thought appeared in her head. Annie remembered him sharing his favorite Bible story about Jonah and the whale. That ole Gator Nick haunted the swamps that Brimstone Pete crossed to check his traps and preach to lost souls. Ole Nick had teeth like crosscut saws and was forty feet long, from tail to jaws. "That ole Gator Nick! I must go and see him real quick!" thought Annie. So, she geared up and headed out into the swamp, looking for Gator Nick. She was sure he must have eaten Peter, as that was the only possible explanation for why he had not returned home. A horrifying thought.

Annie built a fire that very night and summoned the powers of her second sight. She ran alone into the swamps, the dark, dismal deep; in stillness, she focused, so she could find her beloved Pete. Three weeks in, she found Gator Nick all right, and they scrapped and brawled and had a terrible fight. Annie snapped his jaw and broke it with her bare hands; Ole Nick's dying tremble shook the bayou lands.

Right then and there, Annie took her knife and gutted Ole Nick open wide. She searched for Pete from head to tail, but no sign of Pete remained inside. Suddenly, she noticed Pete's bible. His holy book was still intact. It was in perfect shape, as if it had been preserved under glass.

The oak and cypress trees mourned Annie's loss; their weeping could be heard through the thick Spanish moss. And then silence fell over every rock, limb, and leaf, and in a swamp that's mighty quiet. The old folks say that when Ole Nick died, Satan left the earth that day to hide. No one ever sinned again, and the crops grew bigger than ever before. But that didn't comfort Annie; her grief was so intense, her once-warm heart grew cold. She found some comfort in the twenty-third Psalm, but even that wasn't a strong enough antidote for her broken heart. So, she closed her door to the outside world, never to open it again.

While Annie Christmas may have decided to exit this world in a tragic way, when the door closed to her folklore, another door opened in Voudou's world of the Invisibles. There, she is the patron ancestral spirit that empowers women. There, she lives on in infamy. There, Annie Christmas remains a mystery among Mysteries.

A conjure woman throwing wanga in the swamp.

2

Aunt Julia Brown: Voudou Legend or Hoodoo Curse?

When I Die, I'm Gonna Take the Whole Town with Me!

—AUNT JULIA BROWN

S he was their healer and midwife, and the townsfolk utilized every bit of her services, whether it was to fight a cold or to help women give birth. Aunt Julia Brown could also be counted on for her magickal services, and she created little charms to mend relationships and bring good luck in games of chance. She told fortunes, too, and though people usually paid attention to her, toward the end of her life, that changed.

She tried to warn folks, but the community didn't pay her any attention. So, the death toll grew. According to the *Wichita Beacon* on September 30, 1915, "Seven or eight white people and seventeen negroes were drowned and a score more injured at Frenier, Louisiana." Dubbed the "Great Storm of 1915," it passed twenty miles west of New Orleans at 5:50 p.m. Sustained wind velocity was eighty-six miles per hour. The First Presbyterian Church on South Street, facing Lafayette Square, collapsed at 5:02 p.m. As the high tower of the church fell, it crushed two three-story rooming houses on the St. Charles Street side. Scarcely a house in New Orleans escaped without some damage (*Times-Picayune*, n.d.).

On October 1, the newspapers reported that twenty-five people were dead and about twenty injured in Frenier (*Indianapolis News* 1915, 10). In addition, fifty or sixty persons were reported stranded in box cars. There had been heavy damage to the railroad, and miles of track in that section were simply gone. Rescue was impossible. The New Orleans and Northwestern Railroad Bridge over Lake Pontchartrain were under several feet of water (*Evening Republican* 1915, 4).

By Sunday October 3, letters were being received on the hour, describing the destruction to property down the river. "Sufferers along lower river in dire distress—piteously plead for bread crust when boats pass," read one such letter. Echoes of the cries from people stuck on crowded rafts could be heard: "Throw us a crust of bread—a biscuit—anything!" Clothing was also needed, but it was food that was needed the most. The entire town of Frenier had been washed away, and now, where a once-thriving community had stood, was one big body of water—the Gulf of Mexico and Mississippi River joining where the levees broke.

Whenever there are natural disasters, particularly the kind resulting in such devastation as never seen or experienced before, there inevitably arises questions of an existential nature. How did this happen? Why did this happen? Why this community? Why us? In the case of the Great Storm of 1915, when all rational explanations failed, some folks looked to the supernatural to explain their misfortune. They blamed it on the local Voudou priestess, Aunt Julia Brown. She had sung a little ditty about it, after all.

Julia Brown is sometimes referred to as Julia White or Julia Black. It doesn't much matter what color her last name is because everyone knows who you are talking about when you mention the Voudou Queen from Frenier, Louisiana, and the Great Flood of 1915. She was well-respected and had a great deal of influence in the swamp communities.

The small town of Frenier was originally settled by German immigrants in 1850. The town was called La Frenier, after Nicholas Chauvin de La

Frenier, the attorney general for Louisiana at the time. By 1915, there were several hundred people living there. Frenier is surrounded by the Manchac Swamp, which is composed of swamplands located about a half an hour from New Orleans.

Aunt Julia Brown was not from Frenier originally. According to census records, she was born in the Gentilly neighborhood of New Orleans sometime in 1845 as Julia Bernard. Her parents were both born in Maryland. In 1882, she married Celistine "Celis" Brown, who was born in Texas. They had five children together, three of whom survived to adulthood: Matilda, Senorina, and William.

About twenty years after their marriage, the federal government gave Celis a forty-acre homestead plot to farm, property that likely passed on to Julia after his death around 1914. This plot of land comprised the majority of the town of Frenier.

Because Julia held title to nearly the entire town, the locals there held her in high regard. Furthermore, her knowledge of the healing qualities of the local herbs and roots and her skill in their application made her services coveted by the townsfolk. In Frenier, if someone got seriously injured or ill, they could either pay twenty-five cents to ride the train to New Orleans that only came once or twice a week or go to Aunt Julia Brown for treatment. Of course, most opted to stay in town and see Aunt Julia Brown. I mean, it was convenient and logical. And, apparently, she was exceptionally good at what she did.

In addition to serving the needs of the people of Frenier, Aunt Julia Brown also tended to the needs of those people living in the nearby community of Ruddock. At some point, however, the townsfolk began taking Aunt Julia Brown for granted. They expected her to help them no matter what and often without pay. They considered her a prophetess and went to her to have their fortunes told, as well as to buy her powerful Voudou charms. Between her magick, fortune-telling, and healing activities, she had no personal time.

So, to dissuade folks from overstaying their welcome, Aunt Julia Brown started telling them about bad things that were going to happen in the future. People didn't like the change in her personality and that, combined with the dread of her fortunes, caused them to avoid her. Their disrespect offended her and made her angry. As time went on and she had no one to talk to, Aunt Julia Brown's resentment festered. She began talking to herself, making her seem even crazier to her neighbors.

Well, Aunt Julia Brown was a musician, and it was not uncommon for people to hear her sing and play the guitar. Legend says that sometime in 1915, she had a premonition of her own death. She could be heard talking to herself about it. She even sang a song about it for all to hear: "When I die, I'm gonna take the whole town with me." This really freaked them out, as they believed she was cursing them.

Unfortunately, they may have been correct. They were about to find out, once and for all, exactly how powerful that ole Voudou Queen really was.

Sadly, on September 28, 1915, Aunt Julia Brown died of natural causes at the age of seventy. On October 2, 1915, the *Times-Picayune* described her funeral on the day of the storm:

> Many pranks were played by wind and tide. Negroes had gathered for miles around to attend the funeral of "Aunt" Julia Brown, an old negress who was well known in that section and was a big property owner. The funeral was scheduled . . . and "Aunt" Julia had been placed in her casket and the casket in turn had been placed in the customary wooden box and sealed. At 4 o'clock, however, the storm had become so violent that the negroes left the house in a stampede, abandoning the corpse. The corpse was found Thursday and so was the wooden box, but the casket never has been found.

According to legend, the entire town attended Aunt Julia Brown's funeral in the hopes she would look favorably upon them after her passing. The memorial service took place on September 29, the very day that the New Orleans hurricane of 1915 struck. The Category 4 storm swept through Louisiana as the nails were being hammered into her coffin, flattening small towns like Frenier in its path. Without a proper weather prediction system, no one saw it coming. All of the townsfolk reportedly died except for two people who had left Frenier for the day.

While there is the common legend of Aunt Julia Brown placing a curse on the townspeople with her song, most folks don't remember her that way. She was beloved by them, and they don't believe she would act with malicious intent toward them, even if she were annoyed at them or had perhaps felt disrespected. Instead of a curse, they choose to believe she issued a warning when she sang her song.

The survivors of the Great Storm of 1915 created the Frenier cemetery in the Manchac Swamp where the town once stood. Later, they erected a fence and randomly placed grave markers to give a sense of containment to the tragedy. Separated from the others by about one hundred yards is Aunt Julia Brown's grave marker.

Since the graveyard is now on private land, it is no longer accessible by foot or boat (Gemfyre, n.d.). Essentially, the area is a mass grave consisting of an estimated twenty-five residents of Frenier. They lost their lives that fateful day, and their spirits are still believed to haunt the area. They say that their bodies sometimes float up from the murky waters, covered in algae and Spanish moss. Most notably, the site is said to be haunted by the Voudou priestess, Aunt Julia Brown, whose song continues to echo in the swamps among the spirit chorales of the night.

Papa Guédé. Mixed media by Denise Alvarado

3

Baron Samedi, Voudou Spirit of Death

Seven nights, Seven moons, Seven gates, Seven tombs.

—CEMETERY CHANT

When most people think of Voudou, they envision a flamboyant skeletal pimp or a red-eyed, evil demon ready to steal your soul. Aside from the red-eyed, evil demon part, that is not a bad descriptor. We know him as Baron Samedi, and though he may be scary looking to some folks, we know him as a raunchy, fun-loving spirit who loves children and dispensing justice.

As the Spirit of Death and Guardian of the Cemetery, Baron Samedi is traditionally depicted as if prepared to be buried Haitian-style—with a top hat, black tuxedo, dark glasses, and cotton plugs in his nostrils. He carries around his gravedigger's tools: a shovel, pickaxe, and hoe.

In Voudou, the first burial of a man in any cemetery is dedicated to Baron Samedi. Like other spirits of New Orleans Voudou, Baron Samedi is called upon for assistance with problems of everyday living. People born on his Feast Day, November 2, are considered his chosen children.

When Africans were brought over in bondage during the Transatlantic slave trade, they brought their gods with them. In the New World, their gods were organized according to *nachons* or nations. Among these nations are the Guédé, the family of spirits to which Baron Samedi and his many manifestations belong. Specifically, Baron Samedi is head of the family of ancestral spirits called Les Morts (the Dead), while Papa Guédé presides over the Guédé. The Guédé are the personification of the Ancestors and sexual regeneration. They are responsible for claiming the souls of the Dead, helping to dig graves, and guiding the newly dead to the other side, where the souls of the Dead pass on their way to Guinee. If a child is dying, Papa Guédé is prayed to, as it is believed that he will not take a life before it is time.

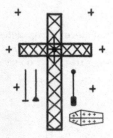

Vévé (ritual symbol) for Papa Guédé

Baron Samedi, on the other hand, stands at the crossroads as the gate-keeper to the Ancestors. As well as being the all-knowing Spirit of Death, he is a sexual loa (spirit), frequently represented by phallic symbols, not unlike the Legbas of West Africa. He is noted for disruption, obscenity, and debauchery, and has a particular fondness for money, white rum, and tobacco, especially Pall Mall cigarettes. And although he appreciates and capitalizes on adult themes, he absolutely loves children and protects them with all of his power. His wife is Manman Brigit.

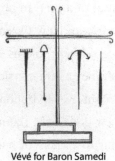

Vévé for Baron Samedi

Many practitioners who work with Baron Samedi know the science of poisons, cursing, and black magick. They know he is a formidable magician who can be extremely helpful with magick rituals, especially those involving children, money, and life changes. But let there be no mistake, he is an assassin. It is he who decides who lives or dies. Though he is feared for his ultimate power, he is known to be wise and honest in his responses to those seeking his help. Baron Samedi is trusted as the supreme lawyer who will make a just judgment when you give him your complaints.

Baron Samedi means, literally, Baron Saturday. Standing dead center between the day of crucifixion, Friday, and the day of resurrection, Sunday, is Saturday, the day that Jesus died. Thus, Baron Samedi is associated with Jesus on the cross. This fact also makes him privy to the secrets of zombiism and resurrection. And while he is spoken of as a single entity, in reality, he has many manifestations, each of which holds influence over certain aspects of death. The most prominent expressions are Baron LaCroix (Baron of the Cross), Baron Kriminèl (Baron of the Criminal), and Baron Simityè (Baron of the Cemetery). In addition to the Barons

are a limitless band of capricious children, known collectively as the Gede spirits, who are as beloved as the Bawons are feared. The Gede are tricksters who cavort in opposition to the senior Bawons. The Gede always laugh, but Bawon never does. Bawon kills, but the Gede heal. Bawon is a skeleton, but the Gede are rotting flesh. Bawon is boss, but the Gede are bums. Bawon imposes harsh order, but the Gede blow it off. Bawon has secrets; the Gede always tell the truth. Bawon tends to dress conservatively, often in a top hat and dress coat, the attire of an undertaker. His face is powdered white, and he needs sunglasses because his eyes can't take the light after his underground work. Typically, one lens is missing. His colors are purple and black. In art and action, the Gede lwa morph into louts, rock stars, black-gowned college graduates, hipsters—whatever's new on the social horizon. (Fowler Museum 2012)

Baron Kriminèl is the first murderer, considered the saint of all criminals, not unlike Cain from the Old Testament. He is evil and violence personified, but also considered a spirit of justice. He resides in the shadow of the psyche. He is much feared, largely due to his unpredictable nature, but Voudouists know that there is nothing to fear unless you are guilty of a crime. In that case, he can be a violent spirit who "runs amok, biting himself and wounding others" (Fowler Museum 2012, 18). Baron Kriminèl is called upon when all else has failed, and the most extreme of interventions is required. He pushes the individual to question the nature of right and wrong, innocence and guilt, and who is judge and jury.

If Baron Kriminèl is given offerings he doesn't like, he will attack those around him and threaten to bite chunks of flesh from the arms of the one who is possessed by him. While Baron Kriminèl is an aspect of Baron Samedi, he is not a popular spirit among New Orleans Voudouists, who are known for their emphasis on healing. Baron Kriminèl shares the same feast day as St. Martin de Porres—November 3—and so is syncretized with that saint.

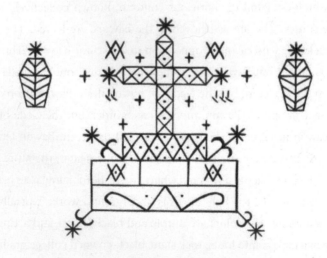

Vévé for Baron LaCroix

While Baron Samedi presides over the Dead and Baron Kriminèl is the saint of criminals, Baron LaCroix owns the graves inside the cemeteries. He is the judge who resides in the center of the cross through which the Dead must pass from the world of the Visibles to the world of the Invisibles. In Haitian Vodou, he is syncretized with St. Expedite.

The cemetery is where the bones of the Ancestors lie, so Baron Simityè knows the Dead's secrets. But it is Baron Samedi who owns the whole kit and kaboodle—the entire cemetery and everything in it, including who comes and goes. All of them and any of them may be referred to simply as "Baron."

It's no wonder Baron Samedi is as popular as he is among serviteurs. Everyone wants a good relationship with the Spirit of Death, after all. He gets to decide whether you live or die. If he doesn't think you are ready, he will refuse to dig your grave and will send you back through the gates to the world of the Visibles where you will live out your natural life. He also decides where your soul goes when you die. You know the legend of selling your soul to the devil at the crossroads? Well, folks get the wrong crossroads' spirit in that urban legend. Usually, the black man at the cross-roads is likened to Papa Legba, but Legba doesn't guard the gates between life and death. Baron Samedi does.

Popular culture often conflates Papa Legba with Baron Samedi, as in *American Horror Story: Coven,* for example. They also get Baron Samedi and Papa Guédé confused. Baron Samedi and Papa Guédé seem to have, essentially, the same job, yet they are different. The difference between them is that Papa Guédé has the ability to read people's minds and to know everything that happens in both the world of the Visibles and the world of the Invisibles. That's why he is depicted as wearing dark sunglasses with one lens removed. It signifies that he sees with his physical eye as well as his psychic eye—his "far-eye," as it is called in hoodoo.

Baron Samedi and his gang of Guédé make regular appearances throughout New Orleans's popular culture, from Mardi Gras to jazz funerals and sports. For example, the football team received their name, the New Orleans VooDoo, in homage to our unique religio-magickal history. Accordingly, the VooDoo's official mascots are known as Bones and Mojo, and their cheerleaders are the VooDoo Dolls (New Orleans Official Tourism Bureau 2012).

Like Papa Legba, Baron Samedi has been depicted in numerous movies, including the 1973 James Bond film *Live and Let Die* and the 1974 movie *Sugar Hill*. These films have been critiqued as Blaxploitation films that promote stereotypes and Voudou as an evil religion. As one article that describes the Baron as presented in *Sugar Hill* states:

> Baron Samedi and the Vodou religion are taken out of context, not only to exploit as stereotypical image of its followers, but also to characterize it as a religion of where empowerment comes only through the destruction of white society. While those that meet their end possess few, if any redeeming qualities, it still sends a negative, unrealistic message about Vodou culture to the general population as a religion based on helping people get revenge. (Paul 2013, 295)

Not surprisingly, New Orleans has its own special secrets for celebrating Baron Samedi. Among them is the legend behind the invocation to enter the Gates of Guinea: Seven nights, Seven moons, Seven gates, Seven tombs. Guinea is the place where the souls of the Dead reside in Voudou cosmology. The rhyme is explained by some as representative of the seven days following a person's death. But in New Orleans, they say if you take Baron Samedi's vévé and lay it over the streets of the French Quarter and the different Cities of the Dead, you will find each of the Seven Gates. Once the gates are located, proper propitiations must be made to the cemetery gatekeepers, and they must be done in a certain order. If all is done correctly, then one may enter the Gates of Guinea, but one's return is never guaranteed.

BARON SAMEDI AND ST. EXPEDITE

In New Orleans Voudou, Baron Samedi is associated with St. Expedite. In fact, in certain contexts, Baron Samedi and St. Expedite are nearly indistinguishable. If you look around with a keen eye in the Voudou shops and temples in New Orleans, you might catch a glimpse of this symbol of syncretization—a skeleton paired with an image of the saint. Often the skeleton, which represents the Baron, is in front of the saint.

For example, St. Expedite plays an important role in the opening ceremony of Mardi Gras. To the general public, Mardi Gras simply looks like a party in the streets—and indeed it is. However, there are much deeper mysteries at play related to Voudou that the average person is completely unaware of. There are the obvious Baron-esque characters and costumes, and a lot of folks draw on Day of the Dead and Santa Muerte imagery. But beneath the imagery is the spiritual, Voudou undercurrent.

Mardi Gras follows a specific procession, starting with the North Side Skull and Bones Gang, who dress as the Guédé and represent St. Expedite. The North Side Skull and Bones Gang is an obscure tradition that began in the early 1800s. They wake up at the crack of dawn on Mardi Gras morning and traverse the Tremé neighborhood yelling out a variety of disturbing phrases, such as "The Worms Go In, The Worms Go Out" and "If You Don't Live Right, The Bone Man Is Comin' For Ya!"

As they parade through the street, they knock on the doors of residents, spreading positive messages like "stay in school" and "say no to drugs." They are allowed into homes, where they visit children in their bedrooms and tell them to listen to their mamas or they're going to die. Essentially, their overall message is the same as St. Expedite's: Do what you can today because tomorrow may not come. Procrastination be gone! In addition to Mardi Gras, St. Expedite leads the Skull and Bones Gang for St. Joseph's Day and Day of the Dead celebrations (Alvarado 2013).

Considered one of the most important spirits in Haitian Vodou and New Orleans Voudou, Baron Samedi mans the ultimate crossroads that all living souls must face—that of life and death. Even though he is the Master of Death, he is also a giver of life. No one can die if the Baron refuses to dig their grave. He is the only spirit who can bring someone back from the brink of death. He is a complex spirit with many manifestations, each with their own funky quirks. His powers are often solicited for curses and sorcery as well as protection and healing.

It's really no wonder that folks get the Voudou spirits all mixed up. There are so many expressions of them that if you don't know the subtle nuances and different specialties of the various Guédé, they will all look and sound alike. To a nonpractitioner, it doesn't matter. To a practitioner, it very much does. Though they are all part of the world of death, they are not all dead people. Papa Guédé is the Spirit of Death. The Guédé are the souls of the Dead. Les Morts are the Dead, they are the Ancestors. And Baron Samedi, also the Spirit of Death, is the upside-down clown who brings joy, laughter, and debauchery when he comes to visit. He can always be counted on as the life of the party.

4

Betsy Toledano, Voudou Queen and Activist

On some articles of her mysterious faith, her honor, as a Voudou,
placed a seal upon her lips.

—New Orleans Weekly Delta 1850

Her story is a short one, but not because her life wasn't interesting or worthy of a longer chapter. It simply means that there are only a few articles written about Voudou Queen Betsy Toledano. The articles are all related to her arrests for practicing the Voudou religion, which was referred to as "encouraging the unlawful assemblages of slaves." The articles also capture a woman unintimidated by the white man's courts and one who advocated for her right to practice her African religion as passed down to her by her grandmother, reportedly a Congo woman.

In the 1850s, there was a notable political concern about the unlawful assembly of slaves, which resulted in targeted persecutions of people participating in Voudou activities. In particular, there was an increase in this activity in the First and Third Municipalities in New Orleans. New Orleans was divided into three municipalities, each of which had a recorder who presided over the legal cases like a judge.

White folks had been concerned about groups of organized black folks since Louisiana territory was still a French colony. The various slave uprisings gave the colonizers reason for concern. The black codes made it illegal for slaves to congregate. It was also illegal for slaves to socialize with free people and white people in organized gatherings. But it wasn't just that folks were intermingling and socializing in secret, legal or not, it was that some of these folks were getting together and doing the Voudou—enslaved, free, black, and white.

"Carried on in secret," the *Times-Picayune* (1850, 2) reported, "they bring the slaves in direct contact with disorderly free negros and mischievous whites . . . to promote discontent, inflame passions, teach them vicious practices, and indispose them to the performance of their duties to their masters."

During the 1850s, there was a slow but steady movement from the public perception of Voudou as ignorant superstition to a dangerous spiritual defense system. Voudou, though touted as primitive, was acknowledged to possess biological warfare in the form of poisons, and any links of Voudou to criminal activity fostered the "Voudou is dangerous" narrative.

Betsy Toledano's fifteen minutes of enduring fame arose out of this social atmosphere. Her private life began as a public spectacle in 1850 when salacious newspaper articles such as "African Barbarians," "Voudouism Unveiled," "The Rites of Voudou," and "More of the Voudous," were published, telling the story of how a group of African American women were arrested for "performing the barbarous ceremonies and mysteries of Voudouism." Toledano was essentially charged with having a gathering of slaves at her home for the purpose of engaging in heathen rites.

At this time in history, remember, it was illegal for Africans and black folks to assemble together in groups, whether freed or enslaved. Toledano was one of the most popular Voudou Queens at the time, so her arrest and the arrest of some of her congregants made it through the local grapevine at record speed. The Voudous showed up in huge numbers, waiting around and crowding the staircases and doorways of Recorder Genois's court on the morning of July 31, 1850:

The high priestess, Betsy Toledano, was described in the newspaper as a "stout, intelligent, free woman of color." She appeared before the recorder to plead her case and defend her right to practice Voudou, which she believed was her religion. She was not intimidated by the legal system, nor was she silent about her beliefs. Instead of denying what she was accused of, Toledano admitted to frequently having meetings for only women to sing songs and discuss the divine feminine.

She contended, in no uncertain terms, that there was nothing wrong with practicing the African religion that her grandmother, who had schooled her on its precepts and mysteries, had passed on to her. She made what was described "with no lack of words or weakness" an argument in her own defense:

> She had a perfect right to hold the meetings of the Voudou Society in her house, if she thought proper to do so—that the society was a religious African Institution which had been transmitted to her through her grandmother, from the ancient Congo Queens—that the performances and incantations, though mysterious, were not immoral—and that, for herself, she gloried in being a priestess to an order so venerable and advantageous as was the order of Voudous. (*New Orleans Weekly Delta* 1850, 3)

The arresting officers present stated that they had often observed slaves going into Toledano's home and singing, which was, in their minds, evidence of criminal behavior. So, when they had heard singing coming from the house the night before, they took it upon themselves to raid the ceremony. According to the officers, the assemblage consisted of every color, "from the lightest tinge of the flat nosed race to the brightest ebony that ever glowed in a cotton field" (*The New Orleans Crescent* 1850, 3).

That's when they arrested Betsy Toledano, along with two slaves, one named Leonora, who belonged to a Mr. Grivot, while the other one was called—I kid you not—Darkey. She belonged to—wait for it—a Mr. McCracken. A white man had apparently escaped along with some other women, black and possibly white. White women were known to love the Voudou on the downlow back in the day. When Toledano's home was raided, the police provided a description of the place, as to be expected:

> They found one of the rooms fitted up as some sort of a chapel. The walls were hung round with colored prints of the saints, the apostles, etc. A number of basins or large earthen bowls were found, some filled with gravel, others with pebbles, two or three with paving stones, and one very large one with a single, good sized, peculiar looking flint stone. There were several glass vases or goblets found containing some strange kind of liquid. (*Times-Picayune* 1850, 1)

In addition to describing the "scene of the crime," the police confiscated a number of items labeled Voudou paraphernalia, including "shells, horsehair, curious aprons, colors, etc." In court, Toledano was called upon to explain what the Voudou paraphernalia were and what they were used for. She was quite accommodating and described many of the items. Toledano said she used the stones to keep the house from being struck by lightning. She said this is done by scattering the pebbles and gravel all across the floor, then the stones are placed in water in the bowls. When the stones are placed in water during a storm, they act as nonconductors of the elements, thus offering protection. As such, the flint and pebble stones were used for "taming and turning aside the fiery shafts of 'Heaven's Artillery'" (*New Orleans Weekly Delta* 1850, 3). Toledano explained that this was an African custom.

Toledano also had a curious necklace of "strange shells" and small "rainbow-tinted beads," apparently given to her by her grandmother, who had acquired it from West Africa many moons ago. The necklace was supposed to give Toledano the power to call down the rain during seasons of drought, and it was believed she could bring the rain down on anyone at any time.

This rumor, of course, when shared in court, became the joke of the day, as everyone in the courtroom burst out into laughter after one person suggested there was no better time than the present, in a hot courtroom, to cool everyone down with a nice rain shower. According to the newspaper report, Toledano responded with nothing more than "a scornful toss of the head and curl of the lip" (*New Orleans Weekly Delta* 1850, 3).

Nevertheless, Toledano was unable to describe some of the confiscated items in detail, as they were official mysteries of the religion. Some of the secrets were to be unknown not only to noninitiates, but also to men. Thus, "on some articles of her mysterious faith, her honor, as a Voudou, placed a seal upon her lips" (*New Orleans Weekly Delta* 1850, 3).

Looking at the information provided in the articles, some of it suggests that Toledano may have served the Voudou spirits Shango or Oya, given the descriptions of the confiscated Voudou paraphernalia. The strange flint stone and concern with lightning and thunder (Heaven's artillery) is associated with Shango and Oya in Orisha worship and Ifá. The rainbow colors of her necklace may suggest Ayeda Wedo, the rainbow serpent or Oya, who is known for all colors of the rainbow. Horsehair is associated with both Shango and Oya. Multiple goblets of liquid could easily be goblets of water, which are commonly found on Voudou altars as well as on the altars of Spiritualists.

After thoroughly reviewing the facts of Betsy Toledano's case, the recorder ended up charging her with the "unlawful assemblage of free people and slaves." Since the accused were required to answer on a future day, he decided that he "required security of Betsy to ensure her appearance at a future hearing on the charge of encouraging the unlawful assemblage of slaves" (*New Orleans Weekly Delta* 1850). It sounds like she was detained in jail until her next hearing. .

I have been unable to locate any further information printed in the newspapers after this time that tells of the final disposition of the case or anything else. At this point, it seems like Betsy Toledano is not mentioned in the public records again. Nevertheless, her name lives on among Voudouists who honor the foremothers of the religion.

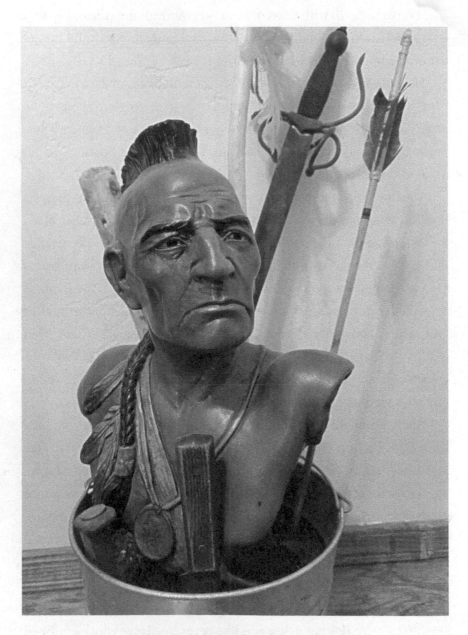

Black Hawk in his bucket (photo courtesy of the author)

5

Black Hawk: The Indian in the Bucket

We can all be as brothers. There is no need to fight with a war of words, or your weapons! For whether you are Indian, black, or white, the sorrow you feel is the same. The love you feel is the same. Your children laugh and smile like all children. Is this not so? I am just an old Indian now, but I think some men forget these things.

—MAKATAIMESHEKIAKIAK

An exceptional spirit was introduced into the New Orleans spiritual landscape by Spiritualist Mother Leafy Anderson at the start of the 20th century, consequently spurring a religious movement unlike any other. His name is Makataimeshekiakiak, meaning "Black Sparrow Hawk." He is more commonly known as Black Hawk, the celebrated war leader of the Sauk American Indian Nation.

The spiritualist churches of New Orleans consider him to be a saint sent by God, and when he comes to help, God is right behind him. His altar space can be a three-tiered altar, a tabletop altar, or a galvanized metal bucket filled with sand or dirt. He is considered the consummate warrior who fights injustices. When called upon, he will come to assist, especially to conquer battles that folks are too weak to fight themselves. He is called the Watchman on the Wall because he sees everything and watches over his children. They say he will come to those who have enough patience to sit still and wait for him.

Black Hawk is revered as an ancestral spirit among New Orleans Voudouists, hoodoos, rootworkers, conjure doctors, and the Mardi Gras Indians. He holds special meaning for each of these groups. To Native Americans, Black Hawk is considered an ancestral hero; to African Americans, he is a defender and liberator. To European Americans, he is the noble savage who fought the good fight. Among his own people, Black Hawk is honored as an ancestor who holds great significance.

It truly is a fascinating dynamic for a Sauk war leader to be put in a bucket, be carried down south from Illinois, and subsequently be embraced by New Orleans Voudou and conjure. Even more mysterious is how he became a primary saint in a new hybridized African American religion called spiritualism. Just how did that happen? Before I delve into that mystery, I think it is important to address a Native perspective about how Black Hawk appears in the various New Orleans magickal and spiritual traditions.

One of the reasons I began writing the book *Conjuring Black Hawk* is the problematic stereotypical imagery and practices present in the tradition. He has been reduced to a mascot and commercial icon due to a lack of cultural knowledge about him as a Sauk Indian. For example, he is commonly depicted as a Plains Indian in full headdress, even though the Sauk do not wear full headdresses. In fact, the Lakota (who are Plains Indians) do wear full headdresses and are actually Black Hawk's historical enemies.

Black Hawk is offered alcohol to "fire him up," even though he hated alcohol and its effects on his people. Moreover, using the terminology "fire him up" is problematic because it gives weight to the drunken Indian stereotype and the phrase "fire water," which is used historically to denigrate Native peoples. Many people stick an American flag in his bucket and use red, white, and blue candles, even though the Americans turned on him and massacred his people. Christian prayers and iconography are used in his devotion by many serviteurs, even though Black Hawk was in no way, shape, or form Christian. These are simply misinformed practices resulting from a lack of knowledge about Black Hawk's actual life and culture.

While most Native Americans are unfamiliar with Black Hawk in spiritualism, Voudou, and conjure, these practices are troublesome to indigenous peoples who are aware. According to Sandra Massey, historic preservation officer of the Sac and Fox Nation, "Without knowing anything about Black Hawk or the Sauk, such practices just bastardize our history and essentially say that the truth is irrelevant" (Brown and Kanouse 2015, 146).

Ah, but the truth is not irrelevant. We owe it to the Ancestors to seek out the truth and align our spiritual practices to reflect an honest history. Spiritual practices can change to accommodate all sorts of things, and I believe that some of these practices will change with education. I teach my students who are devotees of Black Hawk an accurate history and more culturally acceptable practices for devotion. For example, we offer him actual water instead of alcohol, as water is the most important medicine in the Indian worldview. We do away with the American flag because the point of being a devotee is to honor his spirit not disrespect him with symbols of oppression. We use actual images of Black Hawk instead of depicting him as his enemy in full headdress. We avoid Christian practices in his service because the imposition of Christianity on Native peoples has been culturally catastrophic, and Black Hawk was not Christian. A willingness to honor his legacy truthfully can remedy many of the problematic practices. Individuals resistant to these kinds of changes should and must question their motives.

In addition to acknowledging the issues from a Native perspective, it behooves us to remember that Black Hawk servitude is, in essence, a hybrid spiritual tradition, whether it is found in spiritualism, Voudou, or conjure. There are elements of both African and Native cultures present in each. So, we continue this chapter with the question: Just who is Black

Hawk, and how did he end up in the pantheon of a matriarchal, African American religion? What's more, how did he end up in New Orleans? To answer this mystery, we need to look at some basic facts about Black Hawk, the man. We also need to learn about Leafy Anderson, the Reverend Mother of the Spiritualist Church, and her successors. She brought Black Hawk as a spirit guide to New Orleans from Chicago in 1918, and her successors continued the tradition of Black Hawk devotion after her passing.

BLACK HAWK'S LIFE, CELEBRITY, AND DEATH

Black Hawk was born in 1767 at Saukenuk, the Sauk tribe's principal city, located along the Rock River. He was born into the Thunder clan. He chose to have only one wife, Asshewequa (Singing Bird), even though in Sauk culture, polygamy was the norm. "This is the only wife I ever had or will ever have. She is a good woman and teaches my boys to be brave" (Black Hawk [1833] 1882, 41). Black Hawk and Singing Bird had five children—two girls and three boys. One of his sons, Waupekuk (White Fox), was adopted.

Black Hawk was an appointed war chief who inherited his clan's sacred medicine bundle from his father, Pyesa, who was a medicine man. As such, he was charged with protecting the "Soul of the Nation." It was a responsibility of the highest spiritual honor.

When he was young, Black Hawk witnessed his father being killed by the Cherokee, and he never forgot it. "The loss of my father, by the Cherokees, has made me anxious to avenge his death by the annihilation of all their race" (Black Hawk [1833] 1882, 50). He was so devastated by the loss that he gathered a war party for the express purpose of killing all the Cherokees he could find. Black Hawk and his war party traveled into Cherokee country but, ironically, only found five people—four men and one woman. Black Hawk took all of them as his prisoners but later released the four men and brought the woman back to his band to live among them. This was a common practice; to kill a woman was not acceptable to many Indian tribes, but to force her to live with them was. "As great as my hatred was for these people," Black Hawk said, "I could not kill so small a party" (Black Hawk [1833] 1882, 50).

The land inhabited by the Sac[3] and Fox above the mouth of the Rock River in the Mississippi was a beloved area for Black Hawk and his people. At one time, they had more than eight hundred acres cultivated for beans, corn, pumpkins, and squash there. It was home to more than one thousand families. Black Hawk grew up there, having a sacred reverence for the land. He provided for his family and protected his community from the Osage and the Lakota who lived on the other side of the Mississippi River.

In his autobiography, Black Hawk recalled it fondly. Then, he told of an evil spirit taking over the land, no doubt representing his feelings about the effects of war with white people on his ancestral land. "It was our garden," said Black Hawk, "supplying us with strawberries, blackberries, gooseberries, plums, apples, and nuts of different kinds" ([1833] 1882, 57). He continued:

> In my early life, I spent many happy days on this island. A good spirit had charge of it, which lived in a cave immediately under the place where the fort now stands. This guardian spirit has often been seen by our people. It was white, with large wings like a swan's, but ten times larger. We were particular not to make much noise in that part of the island which it inhabited for fear of disturbing it. But the noise at the fort has since driven it away, and no doubt a bad spirit has taken its place. ([1833] 1882, 57)

There were several battles in which Black Hawk fought, though it is the so-called Black Hawk War of 1832 that made him famous. To be clear, Black Hawk did his best to avoid war with the whites. He was willing to

---

3   The spelling "Sauk" is used by the tribe, while "Sac" is the designated spelling used by the government to denote the merging of the two tribes (Sac and Fox) for treaty-making purposes.

live in peace, but he saw them steal his people's land, and that did not sit right with him. He did not understand the concept of owning land. It was not the Indian way for one person in a tribe to represent an entire nation of communities. And though the whites blamed the Indians for instigating the war, that is not what actually happened.

Sac and Fox land spanned a large territory, encompassing much of Iowa and Wisconsin. In 1804, treaties were being brokered by the Feds, and whites were encroaching on Indian territory. Black Hawk tells of an incident in his autobiography when one of his people killed an American found hunting on Sauk territory. That didn't sit well with then territorial governor, William Henry Harrison, who confined the Indian in the St. Louis prison for the offense.

To prevent war, the Sauk sent a group of representatives with a prisoner for a swap. A mere swap was insufficient to the Americans, so they convinced the Sauk to sign a treaty ceding control of fifteen million acres (!) to the federal government in exchange for the offender's release. The treaty of 1804 gave the Sauk the "privilege of living and hunting" on the lands, but as more and more white families moved in and set up home, conflict grew between the Indians and the whites. There were many Indians who resisted the treaty and a lot of whites who did not like sharing their space with the Indians.

Adding insult to injury, the Sauk prisoner was shot dead when he was released! Not only was it an unfairly brokered deal, but the Americans didn't even honor their part of it. These events fueled an ever-growing population of dissenters among the Sauk.

During the War of 1812, Black Hawk fought with the British and later joined in the attack on Fort Madison. Years later, when he returned home from a hunt, he found that his home had been divvied up among white settlers after they had destroyed his corn crops. Black Hawk never dreamed in a million years that the whites would take over his village, of all places. He saw that they had plenty of land. Why would they need his home, too? But they did; they forced him from his homeland, and his people began to starve.

Black Hawk was between a rock and a hard place. He was facing a whole slew of Illinois militiamen and was outnumbered. Instead of leading his braves to a slaughter, he was forced to sign yet another absurd agreement in which he had to promise not to return to their ancestral lands without prior consent by the government. Though they were promised corn to replace the destroyed crops, by winter, Black Hawk and his followers were starving to death. Corn doesn't grow in the Midwest in wintertime.

Accompanied by women, children, and elders, Black Hawk traveled north from his home village and sought help from his Winnebago neighbors. Black Hawk also decided to send a party of three Indians with a flag of peace to the other side of the river where the American soldiers were. He knew he was outnumbered, and his people were weak and hungry. Two drunken guards mistook their approach as hostile and killed them.

This was the start of the so-called Black Hawk War. In retaliation, Black Hawk sent forty braves to attack 270 white soldiers, killing a dozen in the process. He took the Sauk women, children, and elders to Lake Koshkonong, where they would be safe. Black Hawk then led his warriors into war in Illinois, where they were met by Federal troops and the state militia, who drove them back into Wisconsin, where some mining rangers lay in wait. Clearly outnumbered, Black Hawk attempted to surrender, but in the end, it was complete bedlam.

After the war, Black Hawk was captured and taken to the eastern United States and imprisoned. After several months, he, his two remaining sons, Whirling Thunder (Nasheaskuk) and Tommy Hawk (Gamesett, aka Nasomsee Roaring Thunder), and three others were summoned by President Andrew Jackson. President Jackson promised them freedom if they agreed to cease fighting. As a bonus, the president decided to give them a "tour" of the growing civilization.

It was clearly meant to be a dog and pony show intended to humiliate the captive Indians. However, Black Hawk's reputation preceded him. The media were fixated on the "noble savages," following their every move and spinning stories out of everything that even hinted of being newsworthy. They reported on gossip with the same ardent fervor that drives contemporary paparazzi.

News reporters were surprised to find Black Hawk quite approachable. They adored Whirling Thunder, whom they characterized as very handsome and fancied by white women. They even coined the name "Handsome Jack" when referencing him. There were enough newspapers hostile to President Jackson to create a media frenzy around Black Hawk that took him from prisoner of war to darling of the press. President Jackson took pains to avoid traveling to cities where he would have to share in the publicity. Despite his best efforts, President Jackson's plan for a humiliation tour backfired as Black Hawk and his comrades became instant celebrities. This unexpected turn of events incensed President Jackson, and the phenomenon was referred to as "Blackhawkiana."

Black Hawk eventually settled in a small rural town in Wisconsin near the Iowa River. In 1834, he dictated his life story to a government interpreter named Antoine LeClaire. It was published and became one of the most important pieces of ethnographic literature of all time, in my humble opinion. Black Hawk became ill in the fall of 1838 and died at age seventy-one on October 3 of the same year in southeastern Iowa.

Black Hawk had previously picked out the spot to be his burial site on James Jordan's farm in Iowaville. While he was sick, his wife, Singing Bird, is said to have been very devoted. He was tended to in his final days by his wife and family and his tribe's medicine man. When the time was inevitable, Singing Bird noted his advanced age and that Manitou (meaning "Great Spirit") had called him home.

"You are old, and must soon die, for the Manitou has called you."
—SINGING BIRD

Immediately upon his death, Black Hawk was buried according to the tradition of his people. He was laid in a shallow hole in the ground in a seated posture, with most of his body from the waist up above ground, his hands grasping his cane. A sword was laid beside him. The part of his body above ground was covered by the frock coat he had received while in Washington, DC, some six years earlier. Draped around his neck were three of his favorite medallions that he had received from important dignitaries during his lifetime. One medallion had an image of Andrew Jackson and another of James Madison. The third he had received from the city of Boston.

To assist him in his journey to the spirit world were a pair of moccasins and three days' worth of food. A trench about eight feet square was dug around the grave. In this trench was set picketing about eight feet high, which secured the grave against wild animals. A pole with the American flag was also erected.

Ironically, Black Hawk's remains did not need to be protected from wild animals but from people who coveted his bones. Within a year after his burial, on July 3, 1839, Black Hawk's head—which had fallen off his body—was stolen by a Dr. Turner and his accomplices. They later stole his corpse and took it to Quincy, Illinois. They threw Black Hawk's body into a kettle of boiling oil as was done for scalding hogs to remove the flesh from their bones. The doctor then varnished the bones to make them presentable for public display.

All of Black Hawk's polished bones were laid out in the old Presbyterian Church on Fourth Street, where his wife, Singing Bird, was able to identify them. It is said that she recognized Black Hawk from his teeth.

One newspaper report stated that Governor Lucas sent the special police to recover Black Hawk's remains, and they were brought to Burlington to be identified and turned over to the Sac and Fox. However, the newspapers were not forthright in the reporting of this story. There were other reports of "Mrs. Black Hawk" being so impressed by the shiny condition of his bones that she gave the government permission to keep them. I don't buy this version of the story because it is totally contradictory to the traditions of the Sac and Fox, who would normally insist on having his bones returned to them for reinterment. Both of Black Hawk's sons were indignant about the desecration of their father's grave. In fact, Whirling Thunder had this to say about the theft of his father's bones:

> I wish to speak to you about the white people, to let you know that the white people have taken away my father's remains from the grave. I don't like it, and there is not any one of my father's family that likes it. We did not think any white man would be guilty of this. They came in the summer and took away his head, and they have come since in the fall, and taken away his body. We wish the Governor to try to find out who has done it. (Legget 1944, 264)

The story of the desecration of Black Hawk's bones continues to get weirder. It was reported that when his sons found his bones to be stored in a nice dry place, they decided to leave them there. If that is the case, why would Whirling Thunder say what he said? According to one account, his sons requested that their father's bones remain in the custody of Dr. Enos Lowe, who deposited the now-wired skeleton into the Burlington Geological and Historical Society Museum collection. According to this account, Black Hawk's sons visited their father's skeleton on numerous occasions. Tragically, the building was burned to dust in the great fire of 1855. The fire destroyed the building and everything inside, including Black Hawk's bones.

Or maybe not. Rumor has it that Black Hawk's bones did not burn because the individual in charge of them, Dr. Lowe, had taken them with him some years before the fire when he relocated from Burlington to Omaha, Nebraska. This rumor was refuted by Dr. Lowe's son, however, who reported on November 29, 1881:

After Black Hawk's grave had been rifled, and his bones had been recovered, the tribe (Sacs and Foxes) requested my father to take possession of them, and he did so, wiring them, and keeping the skeleton in his office, where, for a long time they continued to come to view it. Subsequently, with the consent of the tribe, he presented it to the Geological and Historical Society of Burlington, and there the remains were destroyed by the burning of their building in 1855. (Snyder 1911, 55)

So, where are Black Hawk's bones? If not burned up in a fire or secreted away by Dr. Lowe, perhaps there is another explanation. According to an alternative theory, his bones were given to a church for medical lectures. Upon the church's demolition, his remains were reportedly buried in a potter's field in Aspen Grove Cemetery, located in Burlington, Iowa (Gaul 2015).

Alas, the final word on Black Hawk's bones remains ambiguous. We may never know where or if he was ever laid to rest.

BLACK HAWK'S SPIRIT COMES TO NEW ORLEANS

New Orleans provided fertile ground for the arrival and acceptance of a spirit such as Black Hawk into her cultural and spiritual landscape. Several syncretic traditions of Africans and American Indians were already in place at the time of his introduction, including the West and Central African–influenced Voudou religion and the Mardi Gras Indians, aka Black Indians or Mardi Gras Black Indians.

Both Voudou and the Black Indians are comprised of African and Native American elements. The Black Indians can be traced back to around 1848 in New Orleans at the beginning of Mardi Gras, forty-five years after Black Hawk's death and four years before Leafy Anderson's birth (Berry 1995, 48). Celebrating the blending of the two races and the role Native Americans played in helping runaway slaves, the Mardi Gras

Indian tradition set the stage for the type of theatrics and flamboyance found in spiritualist services.

Spiritualism reached its height of popularity from the 1840s to 1920s, and by 1897 it was said to have more than eight million followers in the United States and Europe combined. In Europe and Latin America, similar traditions are referred to as Spiritism and Espiritismo. New Orleans Spiritualism is a New World syncretic faith with Catholic, Pentecostal, Voudou, and hoodoo influences. It is a religion based on communication with spirits of the deceased. Still, it is in no way contrary to the original teachings of Jesus and the apostles.

The Bible is full of descriptions of visions, dreams, trances, and supernatural gifts. On the Mount, Jesus spoke to the spirits of Moses and Elias. In spiritualism, after death, the spirit is free to wander at will and return to visit loved ones, should it so desire to or be called upon. Spiritualists believe that the roses of earth are transplanted in Heaven (*Times-Picayune* 1885).

Mother Leafy Anderson is responsible for the emergence of the woman's spiritualist movement, with Black Hawk servitude at its center. It has been suggested that Black Hawk is not found in spiritualist churches in other parts of the country, but I know of at least one person in California who, more than ten years ago, relayed stories about Black Hawk services there.

According to some reports, Mother Anderson was half Mohawk Indian. Her strategic move to New Orleans was brilliant given the population of African Americans, Native Americans, Redbones, and Creoles who lived in the impoverished neighborhoods where she set up her Church of Eternal Life. The social climate of struggle and oppression was ever present, and when combined with the presence of the Voudou religion, spiritualism had fertile ground in which to grow. Even though Anderson denied any connection to Voudou, the signs are more than evident that she drew from the system of worship, the symbolism, and the pantheon of spirits. For example, there is an emphasis on ancestor reverence, spirit possession, ecstatic dancing, and spiritual workings that employ candles, incense, herbs, oils, baths, and roots in both religions.

In addition to Mother Leafy Anderson, two other spiritualist Mothers can be credited for the proliferation of the Black Hawk tradition in New Orleans. One is Mother Catherine Seals, and the other is Mother Dora. However, it was Mother Anderson who introduced Black Hawk to the Spiritualist Church and to New Orleans, so we will start with her.

MOTHER LEAFY ANDERSON

The mysteries around Black Hawk in New Orleans are reflected in the mysteries surrounding Mother Leafy Anderson's life. Apparently, her birth certificate has never been located, and her obituary states she lived in a town that seems to be nonexistent: Balboa, Wisconsin. However, a niece by marriage, Bishop Edmonia Caldwell, said that Leafy was born in Norfolk, Virginia, out of wedlock, and that she married William Anderson, who lived in Raceland, Louisiana.

She apparently left her husband in 1914 and moved to Chicago. On January 29, 1911, a blurb in the newspaper stated, "William T. Anderson wants a divorce from Leafy Anderson, to whom he was married on June 22, 1905. He charges neglect" (*Cincinnati Inquirer* 1911, 17). Leafy apparently "came back with a cross petition naming one Fannie Jackson" (*Cincinnati Inquirer* 1911, 17). The judge granted Mr. Anderson a decree and ordered him to pay Leafy's attorney's fees, which amounted to twenty-five dollars.

While living in Chicago, Mother Anderson found out about Black Hawk, which comes as no surprise since he is a big part of the Midwest's cultural heritage. She returned to New Orleans in 1918 and brought his spirit with her as her primary guide. Spiritualism flourished in the Midwest and the Northeast, but no church praised Black Hawk's spirit in their pantheon of divinities. Neither were women the prominent spiritual leaders until Mother Anderson began training them in New Orleans. For one dollar a class, she began teaching women the church's rites, including how to summon spirits and the arts of prophesying and healing.

Mother Anderson's church featured traditional "spirit guides" in worship services, with a mixture of Protestant and Catholic Christian iconography, prophesying, laying on of hands, foot washing, and other such activities. Some of the spirit guides found in the spiritualist churches, such as Black Hawk, Father John, and Mary Magdalene, may be found on the altars of rootworkers all over the South and in other parts of the country. Mother Anderson said Black Hawk was the saint of the South, while White Hawk was the saint of the North.

According to one of her successors, Mother Dora, Mother Anderson had the power to make saints. Mother Dora claimed that she didn't know where Mother Anderson got Black Hawk from, but she made him into the saint he became. Mother Dora said Black Hawk had appeared to Mother Anderson and told her that he was the first to start spiritualism in this country before the white man came. After Mother Anderson was sure that Black Hawk wasn't a fake, she took him as her spirit guide and elevated him to sainthood within the Church.

It was a fruitful union of serviteur and saint. Black Hawk stuck around and was amenable to the needs of Mother Anderson and her congregation. She would often call him down on a whim to demonstrate her powers to others, and, happily, he obliged. Sometimes he wowed his serviteurs by announcing his arrival with a loud clap of thunder.

Mother Anderson died on December 19, 1927. As her body lay in wake at the Eternal Life Christian Spiritualist Church of America, one of twenty churches she founded during her lifetime, thousands of disciples arrived to pay their respects. According to her obituary, she spent the last seven years of her life in New Orleans, preaching and "practicing faith healing before a mixed congregation, building up a very large and devoted following" (*Pittsburgh Courier* 1927, 8).

Upon Mother Anderson's passing, Mother Catherine Seals and Mother Dora Tyson carried on the tradition as heads of the Spiritualist Church, relating to Black Hawk as their spirit guide.

MOTHER CATHERINE SEALS

Little is known about Mother Catherine Seals. According to her obituary, she was born Nanny (or Nanie) Cowans in Hustonville, Kentucky, around 1884. In the 1930 U.S. Federal Census, she was listed as living on Charbonnet Street in New Orleans. According to locals who knew her, she was a healer, had good mojo, and played the trombone. She walked the streets barefoot like Jesus and tended to the needs of thousands in the racially mixed congregation that comprised her Temple of Innocent Blood in the Lower 9th Ward in New Orleans.

Nanny moved to New Orleans when she was sixteen and worked as a maid. She was married three times in total, the first time at the age of seventeen, all to abusive men. The last husband beat her so badly that she ended up paralyzed. To no avail, she sought healing from a white faith healer named Brother Isaiah when he was in town performing miracles on the levee of the Mississippi River. He rejected her because she was black.

If you ever want to motivate a woman of color, beat her and tell her no healing for you 'cause you ain't white. Nanny's experiences of abuse and rejection inspired her to start her own church based on her beliefs that segregation has no place in spirituality, religion, and healing. With an emboldened faith in God, she took on the name for which she became famous, Catherine Seals. She healed herself and began healing others. She immediately started an interracial ministry out of her home on Jackson Avenue. By 1922, and with the help of her congregation, she acquired a swath of land amounting to at least eleven city blocks that would become her Temple of the Innocent Blood (Gray 2015).

Mother Catherine's temple was strategically located in an area that was difficult to access to deter those with malicious intent. Several fires had been started by white folks who wanted to put a stop to her activities. A huge aspect of her ministry was providing a refuge for unmarried pregnant women of any race and their illegitimate children. The spirits she served included a Black Jesus and Indian spirit guides like Black Hawk. Mother Catherine served her congregation from 1922 until 1930. It survived for quite some time after her death but ultimately could not be sustained without her.

It's not uncommon for Spiritualists to have photographs of deceased Reverend Mothers on home altars. Mother Catherine can be found in this context, as believers swear she will answer any petition. If you are out of a job, the faithful will burn a candle under her picture. A red candle or white candle in a red glass is set below the image to illuminate it and wake up the saint. "You see, the saint ain't no good if you don't burn this light," reported a conjure woman from Algiers, "that gives life to the saint" (Hyatt 1970–1978, 1:869).

MOTHER DORA

Mother Dora was extremely popular for her work with Black Hawk. She loved him dearly and had regular services with him to discuss day-to-day matters of life. She acknowledged Mother Leafy Anderson as the one who had brought Black Hawk to the South and is the only source I have found to date with the notion that Black Hawk was the saint of the South, while White Hawk was the saint of the North.

In one interview with the Federal Works Project, Mother Dora indicated that Mother Anderson had told her in confidence that "only persons in the South may require special favors or blessings of him" (McKinney, Folder 210); hence, Black Hawk is only for the South. According to Mother Dora, she was not told how Black Hawk had gotten his power or anything else about his life. Mother Dora simply knew that he had power because "he done come and done great things for her people." According to Mother Dora:

> When Mother Anderson first came down heah she tole us about Black Hawk. She tole us dat she wanted us to pray to him because he was a great saint for spiritualism only. Dat is he was a spiritualist saint. . . . Yeah, we had a special night to honor and pay our respects to Black Hawk. Dat night was every Wednesday night. Cose, I use Tuesday night, but de proper night is Wednesday night. (McKinney, Folder 210)

In the early days of New Orleans Spiritualism, some people called him Father Black Hawk while others called him Saint Black Hawk. According to one Spiritualist named Corrine Williams, a member of Mother Dora's spiritual church, Black Hawk is indeed a saint, and she explains why she believes this to be true. She tells how Black Hawk helped her get a job during a time when it seemed impossible:

> She put me in touch wid Saint Black Hawk and Ah prayed every day at 3 p.m. to him. Ah came to church regularly on his night, which is Wednesday. Ah did this for three weeks. After da third week Mother Dora told me dat Black Hawk had been to her and told her dat he was gwine to give me a job. It was hard to believe at first, but she thought about de things an Ah figure out dat after all he was a saint and could do anything. Dat night, Ah saw him. He bent over mah bed and whispered in mah ear, "Child, Ah done found you work, be a good girl and attend church services regularly and stick by Mother Dora." Ah woke up and Ah was scared stiff. De next morning a white woman came to mah house looking for me to work. She offered me ten dollars per week and now Ah'm getting twelve dollars a week and doing fine. Dat's what Black Hawk did for me. Ah'll never forget him as long as Ah live. (Dillon, Folder 029, 1–2)

Fortunately, we have an account from the 1930s about how Black Hawk was petitioned by Mother Dora. She says nothing much happens when she calls on him, except that he does what she wants. "No, he ain't never failed me," said Mother Dora, "and I don't think he will. Yeah, I got confidence in him alright." She provides more details about the Black Hawk services on Wednesdays when asked by an interviewer with the Federal Writers' Project:

> What do I say when I have services on Wednesday night? Well, I put Black Hawk's picture by two candles and say: My dear Black Hawk, I'm coming to you wid all prayers and grace and I think you is de best saint dat Spiritualists has an I want ya to do so and so. Cose, I put me on dere when I'm feeling good. Yeah, dat's all dat's important. He is going to grant me what I want 'cause he knows dat I am his child. (McKinney, Folder 210)

MODERN-DAY BLACK HAWK SERVITUDE

Today, Black Hawk is venerated by several systems of folk magic and religion in New Orleans. His popularity has grown over recent years, particularly among those who practice hoodoo, rootwork, and conjure. He has a fixed place in New Orleans Voudou as loa and spirit guide.

Black Hawk is revered in a couple of spiritual churches in New Orleans, but he does not feature as prominently as in the past because only two spiritual churches out of forty-three survived the devastation of Hurricane Katrina. In the past, his altar might have been a teepee with a plate of incense on the floor, a large statue or bust on a table, or a bust of an Indian in a bucket. Services would be held several times a week, along with an annual feast on December 17. Now, services may occur once a month and annually.

There are similarities in Black Hawk servitude among each of the various traditions. In general, he is petitioned for help with money, protection, justice, legal issues, and overcoming tragedy. He is the consummate warrior who will fight the battles of his serviteurs for them. In spiritualist churches, he is found alongside images of St. Michael, guardian of Israel, and Dr. Martin Luther King. This trinity represents three oppressed races and functions as a symbol of solidarity, strength, and victory.

On New Orleans altars, Black Hawk is represented by a statue or bust of a stereotypical Plains Indian in full headdress. Using culturally incorrect representations of him is commonplace because few statues of Sauk Indians are available in the commercial market, and what is available is vintage and quite expensive. As a result, devotees use what they can find.

Red, black, white, and yellow candles are used in all traditions serving Black Hawk. The colors represent the four sacred directions and may be ascribed other magickal associations, as well. Red is the primary color associated with Black Hawk and represents his spiritual power (Guillory 2011). In addition, incense and spiritual oils are used. Healing rites are primary. A variety of magick rituals are conducted to petition favors from him. Conjure workers tend to do more of these types of workings than Spiritualists and Voudouists, who tend to focus more on devotion and healing than magick.

Because most practitioners of hoodoo, conjure, and rootwork are not Native American, the Indian traditions incorporated within Black Hawk servitude have taken on a unique flavor. As practitioners adopt Native American spiritual practices, some that are not traditionally Native American, such as the use of Indian-head pennies and buffalo nickels, become identified as such. In practice, Indian-head pennies take on the archetypal flavor of their cultural representation. As Indian scouts, like those found in traditional Native American war parties, and Spy Boys, such as those found in Mardi Gras Indian culture, they are used in sympathetic magick to warn of impending danger and fiercely defend tribal territories.

Black Hawk's offerings include spaghetti and meatballs, red beans and rice, bread, and fruit. I like to make him fry bread and stew. He is traditionally served these dishes on Wednesdays and Sundays.

A popular offering in spiritualism and conjure is alcohol. Practitioners justify the practice by explaining that it is meant to "fire him up." Though characteristic of African-derived religions, alcohol as an offering is contrary to both Native American spiritual traditions and Black Hawk's personal belief system. In the context of ancestor reverence, water is the appropriate offering and libation to Black Hawk, as it is the most sacred of all Indian medicines. But, if we want to know Black Hawk's opinion on the subject, we need only listen to his words. Consider the following passage from his biography, where Black Hawk ([1833] 1882, 75) states in no uncertain terms how he feels about alcohol:

> The white people brought whisky to our village, made our people drink, and cheated them out of their homes, guns, and traps. This fraudulent system was carried to such an extent that I anticipated serious difficulties might occur unless a stop was put to it. Consequently, I visited all the whites and begged them not to sell my people whisky. One of them continued the practice openly; I took a party of my young men, went to his house, took out his barrel, broke in the head and poured out the whisky. I did this for fear some of the whites might get killed by my people when they were drunk.

The most unique commonality between traditions is the Indian in the bucket. A Black Hawk bust is placed in a bucket of sand or earth and is used as his altar. His bucket as a ritual object is the embodiment of his spirit in the physical realm. It is remarkably similar to the nganga of the Afro-Cuban religion Palo Mayombe with strong Congo influences. In the Americas, a nganga is an iron cauldron filled with bones, sticks, and herbs that is used to venerate the mpungo (spirits of the Dead). Conjure workers often keep a hatchet, a tomahawk, and a spear in Black Hawk's bucket as his spiritual tools. The hatchet is for chopping through obstacles and breaking the chains that bind us. The tomahawk is for fighting battles, and the spear is for obtaining long-term goals.

Black Hawk's bucket functions as a portal through which he sends the energies needed to help petitioners with their requests. Likewise, it is a communication device—a sort of spiritual telephone, as it were—through which the devotee sends requests and offerings to him in the spirit world. Serving Black Hawk in his bucket allows him to influence the petitioner's life directly; it is a powerful way to develop a meaningful relationship with him using a ritually prepared material object.

In addition to being revered in New Orleans Voudou, spiritualism, and conjure, Black Hawk is celebrated by the Mardi Gras Indians, also known as Black Indians. The Mardi Gras Indians are African American carnival revelers who dress up in costumes they call "suits" that are influenced by Native American ceremonial apparel. They dance and parade in the streets during Mardi Gras and St. Joseph's Day. The masks they don honor the Native Americans that helped enslaved Africans to escape and survive the challenges they faced in the harsh swamps. "Masking" is also a means of acknowledging the mixed-blood heritage of many African Americans in New Orleans.

In the past, masking and parading was a time to settle territorial disputes between tribes in the neighborhood and could be quite violent and bloody. In the 1960s, however, the Chief of Chiefs, Allison Montana, sought to put an end to the violence by encouraging the tribes to put down their knives and guns and take up the needle and thread. He eventually succeeded, and now, instead of violence, they compete over whose suit is the prettiest (Gaudet and McDonald 2003).

The Mardi Gras Indians play an important role in the transmission of cultural knowledge through their chants, dance, and music. There are more than thirty-eight tribes of Mardi Gras Indians in New Orleans, from the oldest, called the Creole Wild West, to one of the youngest, called the Black Hawk Hunters. Noted New Orleans Voudou Priest and actor Divine Prince Ty Emmecca masks as Black Hawk and was the first masking witch doctor medicine man for the Yellow Pocahontas Mardi Gras Indian Tribe.

In a way, Mardi Gras Indians are religious performers enacting specific cultural memories and their elaborate suits are like beautiful altars adorning their bodies. Their costumes are decorated with images and symbols representing particular themes and even portraits and can take six months to a year to complete. Every Black Indian sews their own costume, one bead, sequin, and feather at a time.

As can be seen, Black Hawk is a malleable spirit who thrives in diverse spiritual and magickal environs. And, despite his growing popularity, he remains relatively obscure to the general public. He is remembered by the spiritual churches. He sits on the altars of conjure workers, and he is served by the Voudous. He is venerated in general by the Mardi Gras Indians. Wherever Black Hawk is found, he is called upon to defend the oppressed from injustice. It has become more than evident that he has been adopted by many different spiritual traditions as a spirit guide to whom devotees can turn for help and guidance when needed.

6

The Broomstick Equestrian of Congo Square

The days of witchcraft are returning . . .

—*Times-Picayune*, 1844

New Orleans is not known for witch hunts like Salem is. But that's not to say there weren't any. In fact, the days of witch hunts apparently arrived in New Orleans in the summer of 1844. A great enthusiasm was gathering downtown among the crowd in anticipation of burning a witch "in the shape and form of a negro woman" at the stake. The target, a mysterious old woman with a broken back and a weird-looking eye, was described as "a bona fide witch of the Congo school"—code words for black and African, of course.

She had been taken into custody by the officers of the First Municipality police in New Orleans—yeah, those same guys who busted Marie Laveau, Betsy Toledano, and so many others for their "unlawful assemblies" and Voudou activities during the 1800s. Word on the street was that they would burn the witch at the Place d'Armes at four o'clock in the afternoon.

Catching wind of the story, the reporters for the *Times-Picayune*, curious about the gathering, went down to the Place d'Armes and

Congo Square to see for themselves what was going on. At one point, an "ebony-faced Methuselah" took the reporters aside and solemnly stated, "Masa, it am in my power to inform you. De sorceress will be conflagrated tomorrer morning, between the hours ob 10 and 4 o'clock a.m." (*Times-Picayune* 1844, 2).

You might wonder: What could an old woman with a broken back have done that was so bad it warranted burning her at the stake? And that would be a great question! I mean, this was not common in New Orleans, even with the usual police harassment and increasing propaganda warning of the danger of the local Voudous. Although the Spanish Inquisition had been in place since the arrival of Père Antoine in 1786, the Church was very hush-hush about those activities and took great pains to try heretics outside the city. We don't know how that changed once he died in 1826, however. Well, at least I don't.

In any event, rumors were going around that the "Broomstick Equestrian of Old Salem" had been seen prowling around a man's plantation. Rumor also reported that the witch was "black as the double distilled essence of soot," and had remarkable abilities of animal behavior like that of the hag riders of Southern lore. She was supposedly seen jumping between the cottonwood trees, "like a squirrel laboring under the effects of a bite from a tarantula" (*Times-Picayune* 1844, 2).

Furthermore, she was supposedly seen to frequent the banks of the Mississippi River, where she reportedly performed black magick ceremonies. Of course, these are merely accusations. If she were going to the riverbanks for ritualistic purposes, she was probably making offerings to one of the African goddesses served among the Voudous at the time, perhaps Mami Wata. Or she could have been doing a little fixin' and conjurin'. My point is, we don't know what she was doing. She could have been having a picnic, for all we know. But that wouldn't make for as good a headline, would it?

The scariest of the allegations against the old woman with a broken back and a weird eye was that she could shapeshift and assume the form of any animal she chose. In fact, some folks said she "very coolly took off her skin, washed it in the muddy waters of the Mississippi River, dried it in the moonlight, put it on again, and whisked away to Lapland—probably" (*Times-Picayune* 1844, 2). Some witnesses said that at the time of her arrest, she had just slipped out of her skin when someone put salt on it so she couldn't put it back on. It had the effect of rendering it "raw as a piece of beef" (*Baton Rouge Gazette* 1844).

Rumors of the witch spread among the market women like wildfire. The mayor's office was soon packed with people demanding answers about when the execution would occur. The reporting does not indicate how many folks were demanding her release or requesting leniency on her behalf, as opposed to being part of an angry mob with a blood lust to quench. It seemed at least some of the crowd were concerned that "she had been barbarously made away with." Most were worried that she would be "burned alive in Congo Square at 4 o'clock in the afternoon" (*Times-Picayune* 1844, 2).

Whatever the case may be, "the fury of the mob was intense and for a moment it was feared that they might attempt a rescue" (*Times-Picayune* 1844, 2). The crowd refused to disperse because the police would not give them any information about what was happening with the so-called witch, so the police officers grabbed a hose and sprayed them down. This action finally drove them off from the mayor's office. Off to Congo Square, that is.

Shortly after the crowd began making its way to Congo Square, an elderly woman wrapped in a blanket was placed into a carriage to be transported to jail. As she was getting into the carriage, she was spotted by some bystanders who shouted, "See?! There's the witch!" Of course, this caused a mad rush to ensue, but thanks to the driver's quick response, the horses made their way through the assembled mob.

Once they arrived at the jail, the woman was safely contained within its walls. The only problem was that this person was a decoy, functioning to distract the angry mob and keep the crowds small. It was somewhat effective, as some folks followed the decoy prisoner, but others stayed at the mayor's office, not believing it was the witch who had been transported.

As the time approached four o'clock, the reporters made their way to Congo Square just like everyone else. They asked an elderly woman if she knew what time the witch was supposed to burn.

"Clar to hebin, massa," she said, as she lifted her brass-rimmed glasses from her dull, jaded eyes. "I don't know myself, but I tinks de time is been postponed" (*Times-Picayune* 1844, 2).

Four o'clock came and went. Five o'clock, and still no sign of a witch or a fire. Six o'clock. The crowd had officially become restless as they waited on her execution.

Just then, some folks noticed a woman dressed in a white satin dress with a white bonnet and a white ostrich feather over by the church. For whatever reason, she attracted the younger men of the crowd, who started yelling out that she was the "evil one" and to "burn her up!" Before the police officers who were standing nearby could rescue her, she was attacked. Her clothes were torn from her body, and "it was with the utmost difficulty that they succeeded in getting her inside of the High Constable's office to save her from falling victim to superstition" (*Baton Rouge Gazette* 1844).

I never found out if she was burned alive or not, as there was no follow-up mentioned in the papers after that time. Maybe she got lucky and could be bailed out for ten dollars, as others were. Perhaps she was murdered, and since her life held no value, the papers didn't cover it. Or maybe they didn't cover it because a portion of the population would have objected to the barbaric practice with a much-feared uprising. Sadly, we may never know what ultimately became of the Broomstick Equestrian of Congo Square.

Doctor John altar (photo courtesy of the author)

7

Doctor John Montenée,
Gris Gris Man

Do the conjures. Then listen as once dry dust takes on new life. The facts of history are the bones. Folklore is the flesh. Conjure is the spirit.

—LOUIS MARTINIE

The first recorded Voudou doctor in New Orleans, Doctor John Montenée (c. 1815–1885), is considered the father of New Orleans Voudou. He is the patron ancestral spirit of drummers, Voudou and hoodoo practitioners, rootworkers, and conjure doctors. He was known by many names during his lifetime: Jean Montanet, Hoodoo John, Jean Grisgris, Jean Bayou, Voudou John, Bayou John, Tattoo John, and Doctor John. The latter name is the one that stuck the most.

Described by Henry Castellanos (1895, 94) as "coal black with a tattooed face" who was "negro to the core in color, origin, and principle," Doctor John was both healer and bordello owner. He reportedly had fifteen to twenty wives and is said to have mentored our beloved Voudou Queen, Marie Laveau. He is most famous among New Orleans vodusi for bringing the gris gris tradition from Senegal into the New Orleans Voudou religion. As a matter of fact, Doctor John was a successful entrepreneur who made a living as a skilled herbalist and much-sought-after fortuneteller. In addition, he was a philanthropist who made and served gumbo to the poor every week as part of his ongoing service work to his community:

> Doctor John, of Bayou Road, was supposed to be one of the originators of the sect in New Orleans. He was a Congo, horribly tatooed, and a freedman, although he maintained a glib and servile attitude, except when exercising his "divine powers" with those of his own race. He died shortly after the Civil War, after forty years of amazing power. (*Oakland Tribune* 1926, 74)

Not much is known about Doctor John's life before his obituary, written by Lafcadio Hearn and published in *Harper's Bazaar* in 1885. The obituary, called "Last of the Voudous," is actually a short biography of his life and is the only article of substance written about Doctor John in the 19th century. One hundred and twenty-nine years later, in 2014, the publication of *Dr. John Montanee: A Grimoire* by Louis Martinie made history as the first and only book to be written about Doctor John.

The book celebrates the life of Doctor John and contains conjures meant to elevate him fully to the status of loa. I am honored to have contributed a couple of essays to the grimoire. The grimoire contains reprints of historical documents, such as a contract with Doctor John's signature, marriage certificate, death certificate, and conjures by modern-day practitioners such as Lilith Dorsey, Claudia Williams, Witchdoctor Utu, and Priestess Miriam Chamani.

One of the early descriptions of Doctor John mentions that his face was either tattooed or scarred. He claimed to be from Senegal and the son of a prince (some say he was a prince himself); details he has given about his origins seem to confirm his statements.

Facial scarification and tattooing were prevalent in Senegal at the time and still are, even today. Usually, scarring and tattooing happen during infancy or early childhood and at specific times of life as rites of passage. Designs are incised into the skin by a scarmaster who then cleanses the incisions with water. A prayer to the Ancestors is uttered for protection and blessings. Shea butter, known for its medicinal use as an anti-inflammatory agent, is rubbed into the scars. Finally, charcoal mixed with spittle is rubbed into the wounds to promote healing and ward off evil spirits.

For some African groups, the marks provide a permanent connection to their ancestors. The belief holds that if an individual does not have their tribal scars, they won't be recognized by their ancestors when they die. While there are few detailed descriptions of Doctor John's tattoos or scars, I remember hearing from somewhere that he had a red snake on one cheek and a blue snake on the other. I wish I could remember where I heard that, but, sadly, I do not. I even made a doll of him years ago and painted two snakes on the doll's cheeks according to that description.

In the obituary, Lafcadio Hearn describes Doctor John as having several parallel scars on his cheek, "extending in curves from the edge of either temple to the corner of the lips."

> The Bambaras, who are probably the finest negro race in Senegal, all wear such disfigurations. The scars are made by gashing the cheeks during infancy and are considered a sign of race. Three parallel scars mark the freemen of the tribe; four distinguish their captives or slaves. Now Jean's face had, I am told, three scars, which would prove him a free-born Bambara, or at least a member of some free tribe allied to the Bambaras and living upon their territory. (Hearn 1924, 202)

In addition to noting his facial scarification, Doctor John is described as having ink-black skin, small eyes, a flat nose, and a wooly beard that didn't grey until the final years of his life, if at all. It may have just stayed jet black. He wasn't a tall and imposing character; rather, he was of average height and built like a brick house, having broad shoulders and well-developed muscles. The Bambaras were known for their muscular bodies, and Doctor John represented them well. When he spoke, his voice resonated with authority. Reports by the Federal Writers' Project (FWP) indicate that he dressed neatly in appearance and apparel, always donning a high silk hat and a frilled shirt.

Doctor John was hardly taken seriously by the press during his lifetime. His name appears in the papers only a few times. One article described him as an "oddly tattooed negro" who left Africa in 1839. According to Hearn, when Doctor John was just a boy, he was kidnapped by Spanish slavers, who then sold him and shipped him to Cuba. While enslaved, his West-Indian master took a liking to him and taught him how to cook. John soon excelled at cooking, and his owner decided to free him. Not long thereafter, he got a job on a Spanish vessel as the ship's cook, during which time he traveled the world over. After a while, he got tired of being at sea all the time, so he left his ship at the port of New Orleans and began a new life there as a cotton roller.

Doctor John's imposing presence and physical strength were intimidating to others by just being around him. Not only did he have physical attributes that were superior to his peers, but he also possessed a sort of charisma or "occult influence" over them that made him invaluable as gang leader and overseer:

> Jean possessed the mysterious obi power, the existence of which has been recognized in most slave-holding communities, and with which many a West-Indian planter has been compelled by force of circumstances to affect a compromise. Accordingly, Jean was permitted many liberties which other blacks, although free, would never have presumed to take. Soon it became rumored that he was a seer of no small powers, and that he could tell the future by the marks upon bales of cotton. I have never been able to learn the details of this queer method of telling fortunes; but Jean became so successful in the exercise of it that thousands of colored people flocked to him for predictions and counsel, and even white people, moved by curiosity or by doubt, paid him to prophesy for them. Finally, he became wealthy enough to abandon the levee and purchase a large tract of property on the Bayou Road, where he built a

house. His land extended from Prieur Street on the Bayou Road as far as Roman, covering the greater portion of an extensive square, now well built up. In those days it was a marshy green plain, with a few scattered habitations. (Hearn 1924, 203)

Before the Civil War, Doctor John owned as many as fifty slaves. He was well-off, and many in the upper echelons of society believed in his magickal powers. Prominent men such as John Slidell, an American politician and special Confederate envoy to France, and General Beauregard, known for starting the American Civil War, consulted him regularly about their concerns for the future. "When ignorant people came," reported one newspaper, "he used cards and crystals, but with the higher classes he employed his 'second sight' gift, making at times, it is said, startling revelations" (*Daily Republican* 1879, 3).

Because of his success, Doctor John lived a grand life. He rode a horse-drawn carriage, wearing a "gaudy Spanish costume, and seated upon an elaborately decorated Mexican saddle" (Hearn 1924, 204). At home, he drank only the best claret yet retained only simple furnishings. Still, it was enough to satisfy his numerous wives.

Like Marie Laveau, Doctor John owned slaves. And like Marie Laveau, he seemed to have done so for personal reasons. He apparently obtained his wives by purchasing them and had many children. During the epidemic of 1878, he nearly lost two of his children to yellow fever. "I have no money," he said, "but I can cure my children." He proceeded to do so by harvesting, preparing, and administering an herbal decoction that contained the herb referred to as parasol (Chinaberry). According to a witness, the children were playing outside the very next day (Hearn 1924).

Another article appeared in the newspapers involving court proceedings in which Doctor John alleged that his daughter, Flora, was sold into slavery and imprisoned. In 1874, the *Times-Picayune* (2) reported: "Dr. John Montenée, a well-known resident of this city for 35 years and a well-known Voudou doctor, instituted suit in 1862 against Bertrand Saloy to recover damages alleged to have occurred by the sale of his daughter Flora, who, he alleges, was a free person at the time of sale, in 1862." This article really drives home the fact that Doctor John experienced some extreme challenges that helped define him as the man he was. More than a fortuneteller or brothel owner, he was a husband and a father:

> The girl in question and her mother were slaves at one time of Mr. David Goldman, of this city, who sold them to Montenée in 1854. From the evidence, it seems that Montenée purchased the mother and her child Flora, for the purpose of emancipating said child; that being unable under the laws of Louisiana to have her emancipated, he sent the child to the state of Ohio in 1859, where he alleges, she was emancipated. After her emancipation, she returned to the city of New Orleans where she resided with her father, Montenée. (*Times-Picayune* 1874, 2)

This court battle went on for several years. Before the war began, in 1860, Saloy claimed to have obtained a mortgage on some of Doctor John's real estate, including his daughter Flora, still a slave. Doctor John claimed there was no mortgage, yet Saloy sold Dr. John's property and some slaves anyway in 1862. Then, right after buying Doctor John's daughter, Saloy "caused her to be imprisoned in the Parish Prison of Orleans where it seems she remained six months or more" (*Times-Picayune* 1874, 2). No details are given about how Saloy caused Flora to be put in prison, but it certainly wasn't a hard thing to do at the time. Just like now, you could be arrested just for being black in those days. And if you were a slave? You had to do whatever your master told you to do.

Nevertheless, Doctor John never gave up on trying to get his daughter out of prison and free at last. He tried to stop her from being sold but to no avail. He tried again for her release, this time "by employment of counsel and succeeded before provost Marshall Kinsman in September 1862" (*Times-Picayune* 1874, 2).

After Flora's release from prison, Doctor John understandably sued to recover damages. He presented evidence showing the sum of $435 in expenditures for securing her release, which he was awarded by the jury hearing the case.

DOCTOR JOHN'S GRIS GRIS

Just as we have scant evidence of Marie Laveau's magickal practices, we have even less evidence of Doctor John's magickal practices. So, we rely heavily on oral tradition to fill in the blanks. Far from being an inferior source of data, oral history is the cornerstone of indigenous traditions. In many instances, it is the only means of knowledge transmission.

Nowadays, it is crucial to write down what we know before we lose it. To that end, a group of us have been elevating Doctor John to loa status for some years now. This process has been memorialized in the previously mentioned book, *Dr. John Montanee: A Grimoire* by Louis Martinie.

Aside from modern-day practitioners' personal expressions of devotion and servitude, such as those found in *Dr. John Montanee: A Grimoire*, period descriptions of Doctor John's office exist that give us some clues about his magickal practice. According to Hearn:

> His office furniture consisted of a table, a chair, a picture of the Virgin Mary, an elephant's tusk, some shells which he said were African shells and enabled him to read the future, and a pack of cards in each of which a small hole had been burned. About his person he always carried two small bones wrapped around with a black string, which bones he really appeared to revere as fetiches. Wax candles were burned during his performances; and as he bought a whole box of them every few days during "flush times," one can imagine how large the number of his clients must have been. They poured money into his hands so generously that he became worth at least $50,000! (Hearn 1924, 204)

According to other reports, Doctor John kept a ram's horn on his altar next to his playing cards and shells. The reference to a ram's horn may indicate that his practice included works from the *Sixth Book of Moses,* which calls for the use of a ram's horn to call together the angels and the spirits. In Voudou, conch shells are also used to summon forth the spirits, especially those in or near bodies of water.

In addition, we can glean information about Doctor John's Voudou practice through the few articles that were written about him in the 1800s. One of Doctor John's most famous clients was the slave Pauline, a mulatto who was the property of Peter Redeck. Her story is a testament to the efficacy of Doctor John's charms. It also heeds a witchy warning regarding love magick: it can and often does go awry, so it is rarely recommended.

Pauline was the first person to be hanged at the Parish Prison, erected behind Congo Square in 1832. Apparently, Pauline purchased a love philtre from Doctor John sometime in 1844 for the purpose of charming her master. Well, a year goes by, and one day Redeck goes out of town on business, and Pauline seizes her chance. She drank the philtre herself and became obsessed as a result. She beat Mrs. Redeck and her three children and locked them up in a cabinet for six weeks! She deprived them of food and water and taunted Mrs. Redeck with news of her affair with her husband.

In January 1845, Mayor Edgar Montegut received an anonymous letter indicating a white woman and her children were being held captive at 52 Bayou Road. The police were dispatched to the residence, and there they found Mrs. Redeck and her three children, still alive but in terrible shape. Pauline was arrested, imprisoned, and sentenced to death by hanging. Her sentence was delayed, however, because she was pregnant. Once she gave birth, she was executed as planned. Now that is a love spell gone awry.

It should be noted that Pauline's extreme and violent behavior was not caused by Doctor John's love philtre. It is quite common for people to hire workers for love spells and then not follow directions, and things don't turn out the way they had hoped. In the wrong hands, such as someone prone to obsession, love magick combined with sociopathy can be a dangerous combination.

In addition to gris gris and love philtres, Doctor John was especially known as a skilled herbal healer. He was so successful with his rootdoctoring and knowledge of Creole medicine that people from all races and sexes went to see him for help. They paid him hefty fees for his services, too. Sometimes he did pro bono work.

Once, there was a New Orleans family from the First District, the Krawlens, whose infant had fallen ill. They consulted several doctors who came to assist. Not only did each doctor fail to diagnose the infant's condition, but they also failed to ameliorate the baby's symptoms. They couldn't even provide basic comfort for the child; indeed, it was not for lack of trying.

One day, an elderly black nurse went to their home and told them she had heard about their baby and could make a referral to someone who could help. Now, let there be no mistake, racism was a big thing back then, and white folks were not keen to mix with black folks except under extremely specific conditions. One, they had slaves or black people working for them in some capacity. Two, white men sought Creole and black women for sex and companionship on the downlow. Lastly, white folks often counted on black folks for medical treatment. Creoles, blacks, and Indians were well known for their medicinal knowledge. They often had more effective remedies than the white doctors did.

Well, this old black nurse suggested to the Krawlens that their infant was under a Voudou spell and, as such, needed a Voudou doctor for the remedy. Accordingly, only one Voudou doctor possessed the skills necessary to help the child: Tattoo John.

The Krawlens, desperate to help their child, agreed to the suggestion and immediately sent for Tattoo John. He shortly thereafter appeared on the scene, gris gris satchel in hand.

Doctor John spent about a half hour diagnosing the child using his personal Voudou methods, which were described as "mysterious mummery." He stated the child was indeed under a Voudou spell. He cut open the child's pillow, reached in, and removed a small coffin made from canvas. According to the *Times-Democrat* (1875, 3), which reported on the story, it contained "feathers, four white plumes and a stuffed bird."

Finding fetiches in pillows was a common occurrence back in the day of feather pillows. It was easy to hide tricks in them. What made this trick unique, though, is that it was laced with some sort of poisonous herb or potion. John could tell because it emitted a faint scent that he determined to be a narcotic. This was the reason the child could not be cured thus far. Needless to say, after John removed the trick, the child began almost immediately to improve and, within two days, was as well and strong as ever.

From what I can tell of the newspaper articles published about him in the mid-1800s, it sounds like Doctor John was that era's ghosthunter and paranormal expert, as well as conjure doctor and fortuneteller. For instance, in 1860, a stable on Chippewa and St. Andrew streets burned down. Seven slaves belonging to Mr. Samuel Wilson, who was the owner of the stables, were arrested and charged for setting the fire. But it seems there was more to the story than had been revealed.

At least one reporter indicated that he didn't believe the slaves were responsible for setting the fire. Unexplained violence had been occurring at night at the stables. Windows were being smashed, doors were banged, bricks were being thrown, floors were thumped, and weird sounds and noises occurred in the cellars. People were freaked out by what was going on there. Common sense disappeared, and a supernatural hysteria took over.

The people believed that only one person could figure out what was happening, and that was Doctor John of Bayou Road.

Apparently, a week or so before the fire, Mr. Wilson had asked Doctor John to come out and help with the paranormal activity. While there,

Doctor John was "wordy and windy, and . . . had a great principle, and this great principle was to be paid for—and it was paid for, but the brick throwing only ended in the fire blowing and the destruction of Mr. Wilson's stables" (*The Sunday Delta* 1860, 8).

It never ceases to amaze me the attitude of people who think spiritual workers shouldn't be paid. Back then, spiritual workers and Voudouists were arrested all the time when a conjure didn't work for a client if that client made a complaint to the police. There were frequently notices and articles in the papers with these kinds of stories.

But back to the fire. Somehow, the police were aware that Doctor John had visited Mr. Wilson before the fire. The lieutenant in charge, Lt. Costley, decided that there had to be someone who had mobilized the seven slaves to set the fires and decided to entrap Doctor John by setting him up to be arrested.

Lt. Costley fabricated a story about a man who was hurt and needed help. He sent a messenger to Doctor John, who said:

> Dr. John, come immediately, if not sooner. Come now to the Fourth District; there is a young man paralyzed, his father will pay you unlimited dollars to cure him, come and make him recover through your grand Voudou Power. (*The Sunday Delta* 1860, 8)

Usually, Doctor John's clients paid ten to twenty dollars for advice, herbal medicines, love philtres, and all sorts of folk remedies and gris gris. The above offer would have been enticing for anyone in his position. Once, he was paid fifty dollars for a potion. "It was water," he said to a Creole confidant, "with some common herbs boiled in it. I hurt nobody; but if folks want to give me fifty dollars, I take the fifty dollars every time!" (*The Sunday Delta* 1860, 8)

According to reports, Doctor John climbed onto his horse and buggy, looking like a "disappointed owl when mice are scarce," and headed off to the Fourth District as requested. When he arrived, he did not find a paralyzed boy in the home of a grieving parent, however. Instead, he found himself "inside the back parlor of the calaboose" (*The Sunday Delta* 1860, 8) and taken to jail.

The amount of discrimination and venomous spew written about Doctor John concerning the incident is quite shocking. To the question of his arrest:

> Why? Simply that Dr. John, like many other charlatans, had his "One word to the afflicted"—the credulous—and his one word was about two columns of dry nonsense, equal to "the only first-class literary" twaddle of self-styled and assumed penscratchers, but was not so injurious. The Doctor, too, had, under representations of allaying the spiritual brick throwers, and reducing the ghost market to a consolatory discount, obtained several sums of money in the neighborhood, and at the suggestion of Recorder Adams, refunded $62 to Mr. Samuel Wilson, and, upon this refunding, was discharged from custody. (*The Sunday Delta* 1860, 8)

Basically, Mr. Wilson gets scared and calls Doctor John to get rid of his problem; Doctor John performs the service and receives payment. Wilson still has problems, so he has Doctor John arrested and imprisoned until he gets his money back. That sounds fair.

Despite attempts to shut Doctor John down, he was successful as a businessman. He made a lot of money and owned several properties. He was smart; he didn't rely on just one source of income. He had multiple streams of income from real estate, a café, a grocery, a shoemaker's shop, and conjure. Local lore says he also owned and operated a brothel.

He didn't have any faith in banks, so he buried his money, and when he needed some, he would only dig it up at night under the light of the moon. Sometimes, he hid the money so well that he couldn't find it again! For a long time, folks believed there was still treasure to be found somewhere in the neighborhood of Prieur Street and Bayou Road.

Although Doctor John was successful, business transactions made him a bit nervous, in large part because he was illiterate. That put him at a disadvantage. He did not understand the terms of loans and standard business practices. He would fall behind on payments, and some of his property was even seized to cover debt. So, thinking that things would improve if he knew how to read, he asked a business associate to teach him.

Regrettably, this individual was a shady character. He agreed to help Doctor John and taught him first how to sign his name. Then one day, this guy set a blank piece of paper in front of Doctor John and asked him to sign his name, which Doctor John did, unfortunately. Unbeknownst to Doctor John, he had just signed away all of his real estate property!

Fortunately, Doctor John still had a ton of money buried all over the place, so he bought some other properties. I would imagine that the deed did not go unpunished. Still, there is no documentation of how Doctor John reacted in terms of conjure. Saxon writes that in addition to Doctor John buying more property, "he invested desperately in lottery tickets," which led to his financial ruin more so than the loss of his real estate.

Still, he had his conjure business to make a living, and plenty of people wanted their fortunes told. And his reputation for healing preceded him. So, he was able to keep above water that way. They say he never recovered his fortune, however:

> All his earnings were wasted in tempting fortune. After a score of seizures and a long succession of evictions, he was at last obliged to seek hospitality from some of his numerous children; and of all he had once owned nothing remained to him but his African shells, his elephant's tusk, and the sewing-machine table that had served him to tell fortunes and to burn wax candles upon. Even these, I think, were attached a day or two before his death, which occurred at the house of his daughter by the white wife, an intelligent mulatto with many children of her own. (Hearn 1924, 206)

Even in his unluckiest days, Doctor John carried on with his conjuring activities and upheld his status in the community as a healer, prophesier, and paranormal investigator. He was, very much, a sort of celebrity, and when spotted out and about, many of his admirers would point him out and obsess over his presence. "Dar's Hoodoo John!" folks would exclaim under their breath. Their admiration was understandable. What Doctor John was able to achieve—the wealth he accumulated, the real estate he owned, the businesses he was involved in—makes him stand out as an exceptional human being.

That an illiterate freed slave could accomplish those things is not diminished by his hardships and challenges. Imagine if he had learned to read and comprehend the written word! Hearn (1924, 207) sums it up nicely:

> That an unlettered African slave should have been able to achieve what Jean Bayou achieved in a civilized city, and to earn the wealth and the reputation that he enjoyed during many years of his life, might be cited as a singular evidence of modern popular credulity, but it is also proof that Jean was not an ordinary man in point of natural intelligence.

LAID TO REST

Doctor John died in 1885 from Blight's disease at the age of seventy. He was laid to rest in one of the Voudou cemeteries in New Orleans—St. Roch Cemetery. According to Barbara Trevigne, "Dr. John's relic lies in Section E, Row One, in a wall vault in the Campo Santo, St. Roch Cemetery . . . no. 2225, St. Joseph Aisle" (Trevigne 2010). Currently, the exact location of his burial site is uncertain because, over time, the wall deteriorated, and it was torn down and replaced with a concrete wall. The deterioration, coupled with the destructive forces of Hurricane Katrina, leaves us wondering if his bones still lie in rest or if they were washed away in the great cleansing of the storm.

The unknown location of his gravesite caused locals to find another spot to honor and commune with Doctor John. In St. Louis Cemetery

No. 1—the famous City of the Dead where the Voudou Queen of New Orleans was buried—is an unknown grave that has been designated by practitioners as the folkloric place of rest for the Good Doctor. This tomb is directly behind the conspicuous white pyramid tomb owned by Nicolas Cage. Drummers, rootdoctors, and Voudous of all stripes are known to conjure there. Some even sleep on the grave as a sort of rite of passage. It is as much a part of the sacred geography of New Orleans as any for folks on a Voudou pilgrimage.

Sadly, St. Louis Cemetery No. 1 is no longer open to the public except by appointment with a tour guide due to ongoing vandalism. In the past, when it had been open to the public, you could easily locate Dr. John's folkloric tomb and make an offering. Louis Martinie suggested buying "water from the water sellers standing at the entrance to the cemetery. Pour the water on Dr John's tomb. Leave something consecrated with your sweat or saliva as a link" (Martinie 2014, 203).

THE COMMUNITY ALTAR OF DR. JOHN MONTENÉE

Starling Magickal Occult Shop is the oldest full-service occult house currently in New Orleans. Opened in 1995 by New Orleans Voudou Priestess Claudia Williams and her ceremonial/chaos magician husband Jan Spacek, the shop houses the only official community shrine to Doctor John, making it an important spot in the sacred geography of New Orleans.

It is a hallowed job to man the altar of a cultural ancestor so that community members may make their devotions in a public space. I asked Priestess Claudia about it, and she said that Doctor John's altar was "always growing and a work in progress." This makes sense, of course, for a few reasons. First, he makes his needs known more than usual as he continues to be elevated to loa status. Second, the public has much to do with the size of a community shrine. People visit and make their offerings, and the space must be able to accommodate this. I inquired as to what was at his shrine currently, during the COVID-19 pandemic.

He has currently one dearly loved old djembe drum, one conga drum, and a beautiful old drapo. I believe the drapo was made for Erzulie, but as a lover, he likes it. The conga drum gets used in ritual and he gets drumming every Thursday (his day) for about 20 minutes. He can be most annoyed if he doesn't get his offering of drumming. He also has a bottle of rum and a few cigars always on the altar . . . he tells us his favorite is rum or gin. Though honestly, I have never had the sense he was insulted by or would refuse any alcohol. If it's expensive, whatever it is, all the better. He gets offerings of coins, candy, occasionally jewelry—we never know what people will give. He must have his gifts, or he bangs on the door behind the altar, which happens to be a door to our bedroom we don't use. So, there's no ignoring him. (Williams 2020)

Community altar for Doctor John Montenée at Starling Magickal in New Orleans (photo courtesy of Priestess Claudia Williams)

The shrine encompasses space from the floor all the way up the back wall. Special libations of alcohol stand at the feet of an interesting chair that holds offerings, a candle, and an image of High John the Conqueror. A chicken foot adorned with red feathers hangs between copies of legal documents bearing his name, hanging on the wall behind the altar, along with an enlarged photocopied image of his signature. Priestess Claudia created some art for the good doctor that can be purchased in poster form or on a devotional candle. Of the chair, she shared this tidbit of information:

> His chair is a hand-painted old thing I bought here in New Orleans in the 1990s. At the time, I was not familiar with any African language really. But the chair appears to have the word "Alafia" painted on it along with some very primitive designs. It is very old and has definitely seen some stuff. It seemed a perfect item for the altar. (Williams 2020)

This photo shows the various legal documents and Doctor John's signature hanging on the door behind his altar (photo courtesy of Priestess Claudia Williams).

Practitioners involved in Doctor John's elevation are creating rites and practices as he becomes better known and understood as a spirit. As you can see from the stories of other spirits in this book, they each have their own areas of expertise, quirks, and taboos. They have distinct personalities and things that they like, and they will let their serviteurs know.

> He can be very demanding, but also very funny. At one point early on, he'd heard of this famous person who got tagged, "JLo." He thought this was brilliant. So, his first choice was, "Dr. J." When he heard that was taken by a famous athlete, he was nonplussed. Then came the best one, Lu and Jan and I and Magdalena fell over laughing at this one. He wanted, "Papa Doc." We said, "Wow you have been asleep for a long time." (Williams 2020)

At the time of this writing, we are smack dab in the middle of the COVID-19 pandemic. As a result, the shop is closed, but if you wish to visit, you may do so by appointment. As a commercial establishment, Starling Magickal serves a hybrid function as a point of community devotion to the great gris gris man and as a retail outlet where practitioners can purchase spiritual wares needed for rituals. Starling Magickal Occult Shop is located right in the heart of the French Quarter at 1022 Royal Street, New Orleans.

A NEW CHAPTER

Usually, at the end of a story, essay, or chapter, is the conclusion, the finale, or summary. Somehow, that finality does not fit with Doctor John. Instead, it seems fitting to end at opening the door to a new chapter in the service of Doctor John.

Sometimes, when a person becomes legendary, they cease to be human beings and become just the legend. Doctor John is remembered for his reputation as a powerful gris gris man who was rich and had a lot of wives, and as the teacher of Marie Laveau. The whole context of the trauma of constantly struggling to make his way in a society that didn't want or like him is usually left completely out of his story. This is not only unfortunate but also highly disrespectful. My belief is that his goal, from the onset of becoming a slave, would have been to stake his claim in whatever way he could in his community, find a way out, and do so using his strength and charisma. His internal fortitude and likeability were enough to achieve his eventual freedom from slavery.

I hope that sharing some of the factual events that make up his story moves Doctor John beyond legend and toward human being. In addition to being successful in his various jobs and as a provider, Doctor John would have taken his role as a leader of the Voudous quite seriously. As gris gris is a religio magickal system originating in Senegal, it makes perfect sense that he would have brought knowledge of the tradition with him to New Orleans.

Gris gris is one of the most unique characteristics of New Orleans Voudou and a tradition that persists to this day—Doctor John's contribution to the New Orleans religion is unsurpassed. He expected to be noticed, and he was. His legacy lives on in the heart of the Mysteries and can be felt in the beat of every drum.

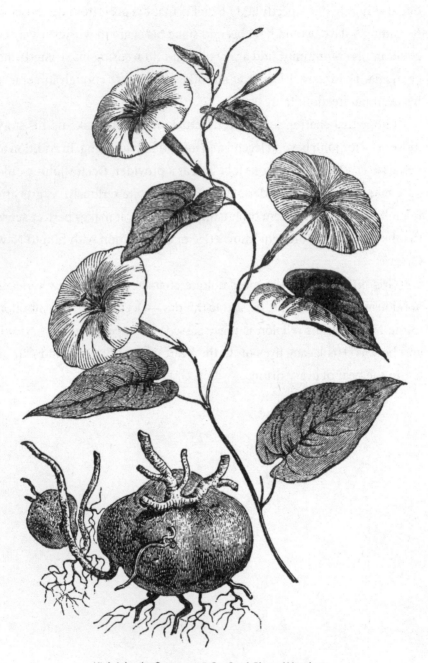

High John the Conqueror © Can Stock Photo / Morphart

8

High John the Conqueror:
Hitting a Straight Lick with
a Crooked Stick

John de Conquer would know what to do in a case like this,
and then he would finish it off with a laugh.

—ZORA NEALE HURSTON

In magickal New Orleans, there are three Johns of spiritual import: Doctor John Montenée, High John the Conqueror, and St. John the Baptist. Now, I have already shared some of Doctor John's story, but now I want to tell you about the spirit that embodies the most famous root of all hoodoo: John the Conqueror, also known in commercial contexts as High John the Conqueror. And in New Orleans, coined the "Hoodoo capital of the world" by notable author and anthropologist Zora Neale Hurston, you can best believe that John the Conqueror has a strong presence.

John the Conqueror is known in hoodoo folklore as a trickster spirit, always making a way out of no way at all, "hitting a straight lick with a crooked stick. Winning the jackpot with no other stake than a laugh" (Hurston 1943, 452). Slaves saw him as emerging from a whisper, finding laughter in sorrow, irony in tragedy, and triumph in despair. He was the bringer of hope, "the source and soul of our laughter and song." He provided much-needed comedic relief in everyday life. He was a resistance figure whose weapons were laughter, cunning, and trickery.

They say that John was a prince who came from Africa, walking on the winds that filled the sails of ships through the Middle Passage. There are no photographs or drawings of the actual John the Conqueror. However, some say he resembled big John Henry, the "steel-driving man" of African American folklore. Or maybe he was "a little, hammered down, low-built man like the Devil's doll-baby" (Hurston 1943, 452). Some say you can't draw a spirit, so quit trying. Others say no one ever talked about what he looked like because it wasn't necessary. White people never knew of his existence, which was by design; they weren't supposed to know about him. He was the slaves' biggest advocate on the downlow, and they lived for the tales of his putting one over on ole Massa.

They say that the spirit of John the Conqueror was around in the form of Brer Rabbit before John came on the scene. That wily mammal had already made the rounds on the plantations for a year and a day by the time John came along. Because he was in the form of an entertaining bunny, his tales spread far and wide. In reality, Brer Rabbit and John the Conqueror are two different spirits, but their functions are similar. Both are tricksters; both gain the edge through cunning, audacity, and intelligence. Both are empowering resistance figures.

John the Conqueror's renown comes from the abundance of folktales describing his exploits. The most significant tales involve his role in procuring freedom through comedic relief and trickery. Freedom was of primary concern to John, and it governed near about all of his decisions. But he wasn't the same kind of resistance figure as San Malo, Bras Coupe, or Annie Christmas. He was good at playing dumb when he needed to, and he excelled at the art of gaslighting. He played ole Massa like a fiddle.

He could make you think yellow was green and green was yellow. He would make you believe that what he did was your doing, and he was a master at leaving ole Massa standing in his place, mouth agape. He was just that cunning. Unfortunately, he suffered more than one whipping for his antics.

As one story is recounted by Sanfield and Ward (1995), John had been working on ole Massa for a while now, and frankly, it was taking its toll on him. People noticed the usually dignified plantation owner wandering one minute and pacing the next, whispering to himself one second and shouting at the nearest person the next. He spoke slowly and clearly and then mumbled and jumbled. He was obsessed with trying to get John to be subservient and act like a slave should. He had tried everything from whippings to ass-kickings, and now he was thinking in terms of iron bits. If a flat iron piece can keep a slave from swallowing, then it fo' sho' can prevent his tongue from wagging.

Truth be told, ole Massa would've shot and killed John just to be rid of his mockery, but his wife reminded him that John was worth more alive and sold than he was dead and cold.

So, Massa agreed to neither torture nor kill John but to sell him instead. He heard about an old rice grower down south looking for field hands, and he thought the man might be interested in John. Massa approached the old rice grower and said, "He's never been sick a day in his life. He does the work of three strong men. If you can get him to work, that is."

The rice grower was an arrogant man and a proud owner of human beings.

"Listen here," said the rice grower. "I am the best slave owner the world over. I can get a slave to do anything. They call me 'Mean Man of the Swamps' where I come from."

"Well, that may be, but you ain't never met ole John. That boy's got a silver tongue that's so shiny he gonna make you laugh when that's not your intention," ole Massa said to the rice grower.

"Is that so?" said the rice grower. "We'll see about that. I'll take him, and I'll make him."

And just like that, John belonged to someone else.

Before long, John found himself working the rice fields in his new home deep in the southern swamps. He felled cypress trees, dug trenches, and anything else his new master wanted. As a matter of fact, on his first day, the old rice grower directed John to dig five hundred feet of new ditches and then split a pile of logs into rails. He even told John something to the effect that he was going to "make rest think he is dead" by the time he was done.

John saw this as a challenge as opposed to a threat. He told the old rice grower that was fine with him but, "if I can make you laugh, will you give me the day off?"

"There's nothing you can do to make me laugh," scowled the rice grower. "But if you can make me laugh," he continued, "I'll not only give you the day off, I'll give you your freedom."

John proceeded to look his new master up and down, circling all around him. He stopped right in front of his face and looked him straight in the eye. The old rice grower, growing angry and still scowling at the audacity, said, "Just what do you think you are looking at, slave?"

John said, "I was just thinking you sure is a handsome fella. Probably the most handsome man I've ever seen here, there, and anywhere."

The old rice grower said, "Well, the feeling is not mutual. I can't say the same thing about you, ugly."

John replied, "Oh sure you can, Massa. If'n only you were as good a liar as I am."

The rice grower's scowl began to fade. He tried hard to keep a straight face but failed in his efforts. He began to grin, and once he allowed himself to smile, he burst out into laughter. The Mean Man of the Swamps found himself laughing hysterically along with John despite his best efforts.

And that is the story of how John earned his freedom.

JOHN THE CONQUEROR'S MORNING GLORY

John the Conqueror was most popular during slavery days because he served an express purpose. People needed the kind of resilience and inspiration he could bring. They needed the hope he dispensed. They needed a vision for the future, one that involved their complete liberation. And when he went back to Africa, they say he left his spirit right here in the United States in the root of a special flower, a variety of morning glory bearing purple flowers. In this way, John the Conqueror never actually left. Whenever anyone needs him, they can access him by communing with the root bearing his namesake.

Although there have been some disagreements about the precise identity of the original plant from which the High John root is procured, it is generally agreed currently that it is a variety of morning glory called *Ipomoea jalapa*. *Ipomea jalapa* is a hermaphrodite because it has both male and female organs on the same plant. That's one of the first things conjure workers and folk magicians learn about High John root. The female parts are nice and round, while the male parts are long and pointy at the end. Some folks liken the rounded portions to the testicles of African American males because they are dark brown and wrinkly! This concept reflects the law of resemblance in imitative magick, whereby an herb or root is ascribed certain magickal qualities due to its appearance. As such, High John roots are prized for virility magick.

Ipomea jalapa has medicinal and magickal value. It was introduced to Europe in 1565 by Spanish explorers as a medicinal herb used to treat an array of illnesses, including diarrhea, constipation, and stomach issues. If you are constipated, it can be taken as a laxative, but if you take too much, it will make you throw up because the root contains a powerful cathartic called *convolvulin*. In essence, the medicinal nature of High John the Conqueror is purging and cleansing.

Seemingly against all logic, the magickal nature of High John the Conqueror root does much more than its medicinal nature. Beyond purging and cleansing, its magickal properties correspond to the folkloric figure John, whose nature was one of conquering all obstacles come hell or high water. In root form, High John is a master root in hoodoo, rootwork, and conjure. It holds influence over all conditions.

High John is, quite naturally, a flowering vine that overshadows all other plants for sunlight and sustenance. High John roots are anointed with Louisiana Van Van oil and carried in the pocket as powerful amulets for drawing luck, personal mastery, commanding power, sexual prowess, protection, and domination. It is said that the person who holds the High John root will be lucky in all things.

Even though John was a spirit from Africa who sought to empower the enslaved, his name and likeness were co-opted by hoodoo marketeers who reimagined him as a white king, complete with a beard and a crown. The refashioning of John's identity may have been inspired, at least in part, by the legend of John being an African prince who was stolen from the Motherland and sold as a slave in America.

On the other hand, the whitening of hoodoo served to broaden the demographic so that more money could be made off African American culture. As Voodoo drugstores took over the role of rootdoctors as suppliers of spiritual products during the early part of the 20th century, the name High John the Conqueror was branded onto numerous products. Many of these products contained no High John the Conqueror root at all (Long 1997).

WORKING THE ROOT

Conjuring the spirit of John the Conqueror these days looks more like magick than devotion. And I reckon John's okay with that. He is the miracle worker, the hope bringer, and shapeshifter—conditions that require magick to manage. The mundane world has ineffective means of controlling the energies of liberation and trickery. Magick, on the other hand, has an arsenal of useful, effective tools.

There are many ways folks work with High John roots. They are carried in a mojo bag or pocket for good luck. They can soak in a favorite cologne to imbue it with their unique qualities. They can be used in powder form as sprinkling dust or incense. But when the root is used as a charm, it requires feeding to retain its power. This reflects the belief that the indwelling spirit—John the Conqueror—must be fed and nurtured to live.

A typical spiritual meal consists of steel dust and sugar, one to attract and the other to sweeten. Some folks will keep their High John roots in a jar layered with ginger root slices. A bottom layer of ginger slices is laid, then the root is placed on top and covered with additional pieces of ginger root. Maintaining a High John root this way is believed to keep its power activated indefinitely. The ginger is switched out annually to keep the energy on a high frequency.

High John the Conqueror is a man, a spirit, and the root where his spirit resides. Every conjure man and conjure woman worth their weight in lodestone grit possesses at least one of these powerful roots and is familiar with its basic lore. It is considered by rootworkers to be the most powerful and significant root of all and is often used in commanding and uncrossing works and drawing luck and success to all areas of life. Whether you know him through his witty stories or through working with his roots, High John the Conqueror is the most famous of all roots used in New Orleans Voudou and hoodoo. As a trickster, he is perhaps the most famous teacher, as well.

Altar to San Maló (photo courtesy of the author)

9

Jean St. Malo: Martyr, African American Cultural Hero, and Voudou Saint

Woe to the white man who would pass this boundary.

—JEAN ST. MALO

The stench of death was in the air, and the horrific end of a successful resistance was on public display for all to see. Three heads were on a pole, and one body of rotting flesh was suspended from a rope. It was meant to deter others who may have had the crazy idea that freedom from bondage without cost was possible. But more so, it was supposed to prevent the enslaved from thinking that running away and murdering white people in the process were activities that would go unpunished. Eventually, you would be found and brought to justice.

For three days and counting, Jean St. Malo's body had hung in front of St. Louis Cathedral and was allowed to rot in the sweltering Southern heat. During this time, his body was picked apart as powerful gris gris and collected as holy relics by the local Catholic Voudous. On June 19, 1784, a martyr was made, marked by the death of a resistor and the birth of an African American cultural hero and Voudou saint.

More than eighty years later, in 1865, this date ironically became known as "Juneteenth," marking the official end date of slavery after the emancipation of remaining slaves in Texas.

Most people describe Jean St. Malo, also known as San Maló, as a runaway slave, but I'd like to present him as a successful resistor against white supremacy and the slave institution of the 18th century. He is famous for leading a band of runaway slaves, referred to as the San Malo Maroons, into the swamps. Located on the outskirts of New Orleans proper, they set up fully functioning communities. Because he was a maroon and accomplished so much as their leader, Jean St. Malo is referred to as St. Maroon in New Orleans Voudou.

Maroons are often described as "fugitive slaves"; their "crime" was the pursuit of freedom. And while some actual crimes were committed in this pursuit of self-determination, one can hardly judge them for fleeing from the hostile social circumstances that constituted Louisiana slave culture.

When Patrick Henry uttered the now-famous words in 1775: "Give me liberty or give me death," he was touted as a principled hero. For the British, the alternative to fighting would have been slavery, which was unthinkable. But when slaves chose to act on this very same philosophy, they were called fugitives and savages, treated as criminals, abused, and enslaved.

San Maló personified the worst fears of the colonists. He empowered other enslaved individuals to flee and pursue freedom on their own terms in the swamps. He created networks of informants, had insiders on the plantations nearby, and even worked on the downlow in neighboring towns for employers who weren't concerned with a worker's status. He could move freely in the world on his own terms, though there were limitations. He was constantly pursued by the authorities, but he believed living free in the swamps was more dignified than living one more day in bondage as another man's property.

AFRICAN AMERICAN CULTURAL HERO

Like the other spirits and saints featured in this book, there's a lot we don't know about San Maló, like his actual name, for example, or what his life was like as a slave. He was last owned by Karl Friedrich d'Arensbourg, a colonial official who led the German settler community along the Mississippi River in Louisiana for more than fifty years. We know that his wife's name was Cecilia. We know she was pregnant at the time of his death. We know he was called Juan San Malo by the Spaniards, "malo" meaning "bad" in Spanish, so the translation would be "Bad Saint John." But it is also said he was called Jean St. Malo by the French after a slave port in Brittany, France, in the city of Saint-Malo. In New Orleans, he is simply called St. Maroon or San Maló by Voudouists. He is believed to be the patron folk saint of runaway slaves.

Even though the environment around New Orleans was wild, harsh, and extreme, it was prime real estate for maroon communities. And despite the severe penalties for runaway slaves in 18th-century Louisiana, San Maló led a vast network of enslaved people to freedom. Assisted by local Native Americans—the Choctaw in particular—he established multiple permanent communities in the swamps, consisting of at least fifty people, half of whom were women.

The territory controlled by San Maló is referred to as Ville Gaillarde and was comprised of the southeastern area between New Orleans and the eastern shore of Lake Borgne (Hall 1992, 212). According to legend, San Maló buried his hatchet in the first cypress knee of Gaillard Island, saying, "Malheur au blanc qui passera ces bornes," meaning "Woe to the white man who would pass this boundary" (Hall 1992, 213).

Fugitive slaves had posed a problem to slave owners in Louisiana ever since Louisiana was birthed into existence. Contrary to popular understanding, slaves were not always docile and submissive. They were always running away and resisting enslavement, leaving colonial Louisianans in constant fear of slave revolt. Between 1719 and 1721, approximately 7,000 slaves arrived in Louisiana, and only 3,745 were counted the following year. How many of the unaccounted for were runaways and how many were dead is unknown.

One thing is certain, the San Malo Maroons were greatly feared by slave owners and the Spanish authorities. And rightly so, as they had developed a highly effective style of guerilla warfare. They were extremely patient and took advantage of the natural dangers of the swamps to take out their pursuers. Whether their pursuers were eaten by alligators or bitten by mosquitos and infected with yellow fever, the Maroons often had to do little but evade discovery or wait until their enemies became so weak that they were easy pickings. Because of the effectiveness of their strategies, active measures were taken to suppress African cultural practices more severely than ever.

In further response to their resistance, Governor Bienville implemented the Louisiana Black Codes to control slave behavior. The codes were supposed to regulate the conduct of slave owners toward slaves for more humane treatment, but that was rarely the case. The codes forbade slaves to bear arms, gather in groups, or practice their African religious traditions. Under Bienville's Black Codes, the weekly dances allowed for the enslaved and free people of color at Congo Square were stopped. Running away was a crime because slaves were viewed as property. Those who committed these crimes were punished by flogging, mutilation, and execution (Bolton and Marshall 1920).

For example, many captured runaway slaves were taken to court, administered the punishment of public torture, and branded on the cheek with the letter "M" or on one shoulder with the fleur-de-lis—a symbol of white supremacy. Their ears would then be cropped. If they ran away a second time, they would be branded again and their hamstrings cut. The third attempt to run away resulted in death.

The fleur-de-lis remains a symbol of New Orleans' European culture. However, its despicable use as a slave branding design of torture is rarely mentioned in popular literature. Over time, its association with slavery has been forgotten and suppressed, causing the people to assign it new meaning as a symbol of unity in New Orleans. In its new, reconstituted spiritual significance, the fleur-de-lis represents an iris, a beautiful purple bloom that symbolizes the Holy Trinity. In contemporary imagination, it is also the symbol of the city's beloved football team, the New Orleans Saints.

For years, the San Malo Maroons managed to survive in the wilderness and evade recapture. Oral tradition says that San Maló was free in the swamps for more than twenty years instead of the more commonly reported eleven years. Under San Maló's leadership, the Maroons formed communities and alliances with certain Native American tribes. They built homes into the large trees, as well as underground. They cut lumber from the cypress trees and crafted items that were sold for cash in local towns. They grew crops such as beans and corn. They used herbs for healing. Women gave birth; many children survived and were kept in the caves during the day to avoid detection. When the children came out during the day, they could barely see since their eyesight had developed in darkness and dim light.

And the amazing thing is that many of these Maroon communities were within earshot of the Big House and even on their slave masters' uncultivated land! They could access the city's resources and evade capture with the help of family members who stayed behind to provide food, supplies, and intel on where the militia was at a given point in time.

MARTYR

The chaotic social circumstances under which the Louisiana colony formed directly affected the emergence of a resistance figure like San Maló. Under the Black Codes, everyone in the Louisiana colonies was forced to convert to Catholicism. However, the colonists did not realize that some slaves had already been converted while still living in the Congo. They had already put a unique, Africanized spin on their expression of Christianity "with the compliance of the Catholic Church" (Thornton 1988, 267). Catholicism's pronounced use of iconography and statuary lent itself well to African traditional religions' fetishism, which fostered a dynamic of syncretism.

Further, there were enough surface-level similarities between the African spirits and practices and the Catholic saints and sacramentals that specific associations between them were made. The Catholic saints were used by slaves and free people of color as stand-ins for their traditional African gods. This dynamic allowed for the continuation of aspects of their traditional religions to go undetected. The hegemony of the Catholic Church "thus could be undermined or shaped by its converts" (France 2008, 219). Renée Soulodre-La France suggests that the dynamics of conversion, syncretism, and resistance allowed for the remaking of Christianity on American soil (2008, 219). I would argue it simultaneously allowed for the remaking of Voudou in America. It was a brilliant, conscious act of both survival and resistance.

In addition to forced religious conversions, the brutal punishments and deaths inflicted upon slaves who did not behave according to white man's rule allowed for the martyrdom of San Maló. He stayed true to his cause to the bitter end—paying for his life in a most dehumanizing way. But this enabled him to become an unintended ancestral hero for all those who descend from slaves in New Orleans. San Maló's wife, Cecilia, avoided being hung twice due to being pregnant.

VOUDOU SAINT

St. Maroon came to be embraced by the Voudou religion, thanks to the Voudou Queens of the 1800s. Marie Laveau reportedly had a statue of St. Maroon on her altar. Raoul Desfrene knew Marie Laveau and her family.

He was a frequent visitor to her home and recalled that she had an altar in the front of the house for "good luck and good work" and another in the back that was out of the sight of visitors. There, she did "bad work." The altar in the front room was covered with a white cloth and had a figure of the Virgin Mary on it along with St. Peter and St. Maroon. According to Desfrene, St. Maroon "was a colored saint white people didn't know nothing about. Even the priests ain't never heard of him 'cause he's a real hoodoo saint" (Tallant 1946, 77–78).

As I wrote in *The Magic of Marie Laveau,* I believe St. Maroon's presence on Marie Laveau's altar and her view of his patronage indicates that her home may have functioned as a safehouse, perhaps for the Underground Railroad. In folk religions and folk magick, specific symbolic objects function as signifiers. In the Underground Railroad, quilts with unique symbols on them were hung on fences outside as a means of communicating with those in need of assistance. There were call-and-response type songs. A lighted lamp of a particular color in a window could signify a safehouse, as could the hoot of an owl.

In today's society, we see similar signifiers in Latin American folk magick. Specific saints act as protectors of families involved in the cartel. A statue of La Santísima Muerte, along with Jesús Malverde, signifies drugs are hidden on the premises, because these saints are believed to protect drug smugglers.

San Maló is the logical ancestral spirit to champion the Freedom Train, given his role in leading the enslaved to freedom and successfully resisting the slave institution for years. No one knows what San Maló looked like, and there are no standard images to represent him. Syncretism calls for grabbing a nearby saint and using him or her as a stand-in for the spirit in need of material representation. Typically, the substitute saint has some superficial similarity to the spirit it represents. In contemporary times, San Maló is often served with candles of St. Martin de Porres, who was the illegitimate son of a Spanish nobleman and an indigenous woman who was a freed slave from Panama. St. Martin de Porres is the patron saint of mixed-raced people, innkeepers, public health workers, and all who seek racial harmony.

Interestingly, there are some references to St. Anthony standing in for San Maló in terms of statuary in New Orleans in the 1800s. One of these accounts is provided by Lyle Saxon in his book *Fabulous New Orleans* (1928). Saxon said he'd always wanted to attend a Voudou ceremony and witness firsthand the sacred rites, but he'd never had the chance. Then, one day—under false pretenses—he got the opportunity.

Saxon had known an enslaved Congo man named Robert for years because Robert had worked for Saxon's closest friends. In a happenchance meeting, Saxon told Robert some cockamamie story about being heartbroken because a rival stole his girlfriend. He said he wanted revenge on his enemy but was afraid to do anything himself. Of course, Robert took the bait and told Saxon he would take him to a Voudou woman to get it taken care of. So, that's what they did. Robert took Saxon to see Mamma Phemie.

Mamma Phemie took Saxon through a variety of rituals that involved uncrossing. She had him unbuttoning, unclothing, and basically stripping down to nothing but a loose white robe wrapped around his body. She then prepared a parterre-type altar on the floor, characteristic of 19th-century hoodoo and Voudou. She recited a litany of Catholic prayers, and she experienced possession. Her style was an eclectic blend of Voudou, hoodoo, and spiritualism, along with a healthy dose of debauchery, if Saxon's description is accurate.

To fix Saxon's problem, Mamma Phemie said she would petition St. Maroon and Li Grand Zombi (the serpent god). To that end, she fashioned a poppet to represent Saxon's rival out of black candle wax. After convincing him to cut himself so that she could have a blood offering to smear on the wax, she placed the effigy near the fire where the gumbo cooked in the center of the room. As the wax melted, Mamma Phemie began praying to

Jesus, Mary, and Joseph. Then she recited the Act of Contrition. Suddenly, she stopped and yelled out: "Maroon!"

Her congregation followed suit, repeating "Maroon!" over and over again. Finally, one of her assistants brought to the parterre a statue of St. Anthony. As he set it down on the altar cloth next to Mamma Phemie, he said, "Done set de table, St. Maroon . . . now what yo' goin' to do?" Immediately the congregation broke out into the chant:

W'at yo' goin' to do? Oh, w'at yo' goin' to do?

Oh, Maroon, oh St. Maroon,

W'at yo' goin' to do?

According to Saxon, "there was no response from the sad-faced saint" (Saxon 1928, 317). Mamma Phemie's attempt to summon the spirit intensified. She rose to her feet, assisted by a young girl whom Saxon dubbed "the mulatto girl," and exclaimed: "Yo' answer me, Maroon! What yo' goin' to do?"

Mamma Phemie stomped her foot and spat wine on the statue. In traditional New Orleans Voudou, this is more accurately described as spraying the image with wine to wake up the spirit. This is done by taking a sip of liquid—usually alcohol of some sort—and spraying the liquid out in a fine mist with the mouth. As Saxon didn't know what he was looking at and wrote from an outsider's perspective, the behavior sounds rude and vile. But it is not when explained in the appropriate cultural and religious context. This is done to bless objects, people, and spaces to prepare them for ritual activity.

Saxon observed Mamma Phemie go into a frenzy and ultimately into what he thought was an epileptic fit. Again, he was watching as an outsider who came under false pretenses with many preconceived ideas about the nature of Voudou, and he got it wrong. Of course, I was not there as a doctor who could determine whether she actually experienced an epileptic fit. I can say that if you have ever witnessed possession in the context of Voudou, it can look like an epileptic fit to the untrained, inexperienced eye. When the spirits are called down, those present at the ceremony may offer their bodies as "horses" for the spirits to "ride." Mamma Phemie had been ridden by St. Maroon, evidenced by the exclamations of her congregants, "She done possess! She got 'er way! St. Maroon done answer 'er!" Her assistant added, "De sperrit done come strong on her!" (Saxon 1928, 318).

After Mamma Phemie came to, bowls of gumbo were passed out to congregants. Saxon was offered gumbo but didn't want to eat it because he saw what he thought was a snake as one of the ingredients. Despite his initial revulsion, he forced himself to take a sip and immediately became sick to his stomach. He continued to watch the ceremony as more possessions began to take place. His anxiety mounted. He clearly did not understand what was going on. He described what he saw in sexual terms, noting how participants were scantily dressed, and "Mamma Phemie was shaking her breasts in rhythm to the drum" (Saxon 1928, 318).

Suddenly, she stood in the middle of the room and shouted: "Zombi!" Saxon then described men and women dropping to the floor writhing and moaning. This is an accurate description of people falling to the floor possessed by Li Grand Zombi. Li Grand Zombi is the primary serpent deity of New Orleans Voudou. The term can refer to the family of serpents in the New Orleans Voudou pantheon, as well. When folks are possessed by Zombi, they will writhe on the floor like a snake and hiss.

After a time, Saxon was given a gris gris designed to remedy his fake problem. "They handed me things that had been prepared for me," Saxon reported. "A small bag containing ashes, hairs from a white horse's tail, salt and pepper, and some crushed dried leaves; a box containing pecans which had been drilled with holes and in which feathers had been inserted; a bundle of feathers, wound around with dried grass" (Saxon 1928, 318).

Saxon was told to take the items he had been given and throw them one at a time in the path of his enemy. The feather bundle was to be put inside his rival's pillow, while the pecans should be placed at his front door. When he next saw his enemy, he was told to throw some salt behind him as he left, which is believed to keep an unwanted person from returning. He was given an orange from St. Maroon's altar to eat to provide him with strength. "It could not fail me now, for St. Maroon had blessed it. Had I not seen this miracle?" (Saxon 1928, 319).

Through this experience—one that he had the privilege of attending though doing so through deceptive means—Saxon maintained a special level of arrogance. His description of the ceremony moved from sexual to animalistic. He described attempted sexual assault, men biting women, and women being hurled halfway across the room. He said people were crashing against him in the dark, and wine was poured on him.

It wasn't long before he ran like a little bitch out of the ceremony, sick to his stomach and scared to death. As he crawled on the floor toward the door, he reached desperately for his clothes and was spotted. Robert asked him if he was okay. All Saxon could do was a motion to let him pass.

"Out! I'm going out! Get out of the way!" he exclaimed.

One of the attendants standing guard outside took him by the arm and escorted him off the property, down an alley, and finally through a gate.

Saxon was so sick all he could do was lean against a lamppost. "Finally, the spasm of nausea passed, and I stagger along the dim streets, back toward a sane world which tells me that Voodoo no longer exists—if it ever existed!" (Saxon 1928, 322).

There are aspects of this ceremony that make me think it was not what Saxon thought it was. Unlike witchcraft, it is not common to offer one's own blood in Voudou as an offering. In fact, it is not usually recommended because it may be perceived as food, and the spirits will want more, make you sick, or hurt you if you offer them your blood. While I have no way to know for sure, Mamma Phemie and her congregation may have played this white man like a fiddle.

First, by making a black wax poppet with his blood to represent him. Black is typically used for enemies and in crossings in New Orleans. This part of the ritual seems contraindicated from a conjure perspective. Why would she make a poppet of Saxon and not of his enemy? All of the ingredients indicate it was a poppet made for an enemy, but she said it represented him. Because Saxon knew nothing about real Voudou or hoodoo, its practices, or materia magica, he had no idea what she was doing right in front of him.

Allowing the poppet to melt to a blob, followed by people and bottles thrown across the room, attempted sexual assault—these are not things typical of a Voudou ceremony. Nor are they the types of activities one would expect during a service summoning St. Maroon. The whole thing sounds exaggerated and staged.

Furthermore, Mamma Phemie called on St. Maroon, who is often petitioned when protection and defense are urgently needed. I think Mamma Phemie knew Saxon was lying and called on St. Maroon to teach him a lesson. Saxon freaked out at the intensity of the ritual, became sick, and crawled on his hands and knees out of the ceremony. What he doesn't see is that group of Voudouists laughing their asses off at this white man who thought he could lie to Mamma Phemie and waste her time with his fake problem. It would not surprise me in the least that she crossed him as punishment.

San Maló may be called a saint, but he is, in actuality, an ancestral spirit in the context of New Orleans Voudou. He is referred to as a saint to remember his heroic deeds and to punctuate his patronage of resistance and rebellion. He has always been petitioned as himself, despite his physical representation as St. Martin de Porres or St. Anthony.

Author Martha Ward suggests that he is syncretized with St. Raymond, but I have not heard of or seen any documentation to prove this association. Moreover, from a practitioner's standpoint, it doesn't make any sense. In New Orleans Voudou and hoodoo, St. Raymond (San Ramon) is petitioned to stop gossip. On the other hand, San Maló is represented by images of St. Martin de Porres, whose patronage is similar, and he is a brown saint, giving him another layer of resemblance.

In every respect, San Maló represents the Voudou underground in New Orleans. For anyone sympathetic to the abolitionist movement, for all who value freedom and the autonomy of self, San Maló is a role model for the Voudou resistance. The Maroons were driven by a philosophy of "freedom by any means necessary," and they accomplished just that. Resistance was central to their philosophy because it was the means by which they attained their God-given right to liberty and self-determination. They did not believe in freedom being given to them because freedom never should have been taken away in the first place.

The elusiveness and general unfamiliarity of San Maló by outsiders of the faith is admittedly an impediment to knowing who this ancestor is and fully understanding his influence on Creole culture and the New Orleans religious community. On the other hand, it is this very elusiveness that has allowed him to continue to protect Voudouists, Voudouism, and her variant forms in New Orleans. As a patron of the Underground Railroad, San Maló's spirit guides and protects, reveals only what is necessary, and never risks discovery and contamination by those who cannot fully appreciate the sacrifices he made for his people.

Voudou Queen Lala in New Orleans in the 1930s.
Used by permission of the State Library of Louisiana

Lala Hopkins, Notorious Hoodoo Queen

Ise don't use it but Ise knows who does. De spirits is mah dope.

—LAURA "LALA" HOPKINS

One of my favorites of all the New Orleans Voudou Queens is Laura Hopkins, known to New Orleans locals as Lala. I had heard about Lala long ago but did not know a whole lot about her. What I did know intrigued me. I love her spunk and her spirit. She was dirt poor, eccentric, and always on the outs with the locals. And she was an ardent admirer of Marie Laveau and a practitioner of Laveau Voudou and hoodoo.

In 1935, the United States Works Progress Administration created the Federal Writers' Project (FWP) to employ historians, teachers, writers, librarians, and other white-collar workers. Initially, the purpose of the project was to produce a series of sectional guidebooks, under the name *American Guide,* focusing on the scenic, historical, cultural, and economic resources of the United States. Lala was a subject under study and participated in several interviews during the late 1930s and early 1940s. This is a significant period in history because it was right out of the Great Depression.

From all reports, Lala tended to move around quite a bit for reasons that are only speculative. She likely had financial problems and probably was required to move. In 1940, she had been living just three months in her little house on North Roman Street. She reported moving to avoid being found by some community members whom she had hoodooed.

At the same time, it seemed a significant part of the community dreaded meeting her even by happenchance. Warnings were given that painted a picture of a frightening old hag who practiced "bad work." Some of the sentiments shared included: "If I see her coming, I crosses da street or goes around da block to keep from meeting her" and "Lala is a devil, she wears a shawl over her head to hide her horns."

A QUESTION OF ETHICS

When the FWP folks would visit her, Lala was usually concerned with basic survival issues. For example, she would be on her way to get rations, her husband's government check, or hiding from her neighbors and avoiding encounters with the law. She made enemies with community members by being a conjure woman for hire; at the bequest of some, she would harm others.

She had a menagerie of animals, including dogs, cats, and pigeons, and relied on her chickens for eggs to eat and to use for her conjure work. Sometimes, her home was a wreck and was described as "disorderly arranged, which indicated an indifferent attitude about cleanliness and sanitation" (McKinney 1937, 2). Other times, she was reportedly cleaning and scrubbing. It really sounds to me like most normal people who live below the poverty line. The excessive criticism and focus on filth and chaos by FWP interviewers was particularly pronounced in their manuscripts.

Catherine Dillon's unpublished Voodoo manuscript is a much-coveted piece of work by researchers interested in New Orleans Voudou and its people. I was excited to finally get my hands on it, as I have yet to see any scholar-practitioners analyze the work. I read each word to understand what was said and observed, rather than rely on second-hand interpretations. I was struck by the utter racist tone of much of the work.

In essence, it is a compilation of interviews, newspaper articles, and other information that Dillon collected over the time she worked with the FWP. In the interviews with Lala, the racist and unethical approaches the interviewers adopted were particularly noticeable. Even "the brilliant young Negro journalist, Robert McKinney" showed a striking lack of cultural and economic sensitivity (Sobol 1939, 5).

For example, to glean information about Lala's life and traditions, an elaborate scheme was concocted by the interviewer, Robert McKinney, and two accomplices representing *Life Magazine,* Mr. Henle from Germany and Mr. Peckles from England. Henley and Peckles accompanied McKinney to the home of a woman named Mrs. Dereco, intending to photo-document a Hoodoo Opening ceremony.

Posing as New York City underworld men, Henley and Peckles said they wanted to make a racket out of hoodoo up North. They sought to gain information about certain Voudou ceremonies and hoodoo rituals, specifically the Opening ceremony and the infamous Black Cat ritual. They were interested in only evil work. After explaining to Mrs. Dereco the nature of the work they needed done, she promised to introduce them to Lala, the Hoodoo Queen, who was known for her "bad work."

The next day, Mrs. Dereco brought the men to Lala's home and introduced them. Lala had been in bed. Her home was dimly lit by just an oil lamp. The men saw a picture of Marie Laveau and a small altar in an adjacent room. They noticed that Lala spoke in a hushed tone when she was talking about hoodoo, as if everything were confidential.

Lala was happy to receive the men but was annoyed when they tried to come off as New York City underworld men, even commenting, "Ise can't see why sich young men want to be gangsters" (McKinney 1937, 3). They laughed at Lala and mocked her even in her presence during rituals she allowed them to attend. The following passage from an interview illustrates a disturbing practice the FWP interviewers engaged in to get what they wanted from her:

> Lala is frightfully ugly, weighs about eighty-five pounds, stands five feet, one inch. She has peculiar looking black eyes that semi-wink every time she talks. . . . We offered to buy her some dope because she looked like a dope addict, but she refused it, stating, "Ise don't use it but Ise knows who does. De spirits is mah dope." (McKinney 1937, 2)

Offering drugs to an informant because she "looked like a dope addict" is disgraceful from a researcher's perspective and even more so as a practitioner of the faith. McKinney, Henley, and Peckles emerged from their attempts with some valuable information; though, not everything they wanted. Lala may have been poor and illiterate, but she had more street smarts than all interviewers with the Federal Writers' Project combined.

MARIE LAVEAU DEVOTEE

Whenever Lala was visited by someone to discuss her services and practices, she always made a point of acknowledging the mother of New Orleans Voudou, Marie Laveau. "She showed us a newspaper clipping of Marie Laveau," McKinney writes. "Lala is a great admirer of the former hoodoo Queen" (McKinney 1937, 2). According to Lala:

> I love Marie Laveau. I go an' put flowers on her grave an' she help me too, yeah—I tell jes' yo' dis, so don' yo' tell nobody. She taught me all I know. When I was a little girl, I used to go to her house on St. Ann street

and I'd peep in an' watch her, den she taught me all I know 'cause I was born wid a veil an' dat's why I can do somethings an' I'm good. Yes, I'm good, but not like Marie Laveau! No, she was a crack—but I tell yo' what I can do, I can make de candle have five fingers . . . yes, me! An' if de chickens had laid a egg today, I'd make it walk fo' yo'. Yes, I done plenty, but I'm not good like Marie Laveau. (Wallace 1940, 2)

In my book, *The Magic of Marie Laveau*, I described how Lala empowered her magick with help from the Voudou Queen. She kept a small altar in the corner of her room with a framed image of Marie Laveau she had procured by cutting it out of the newspaper. Lala was said to set workings in front of Marie Laveau's image and pray: "Marie, yo' da greatest—yo' help me do my work" (Wallace 1940, 3).

Perhaps the most telling sign of the depth of Lala's devotion to Marie Laveau is seen when she was visited by two rich, white, French ladies one day. She was very grateful for the business opportunity and was celebrating with her sister and the women. They had purchased some beer to drink for the occasion, but Lala didn't drink any. Instead, she walked throughout her home, pouring beer on the floor as a libation to her beloved Voudou Queen:

Know what I'm doing? Payin' off, dat's what. Come on, ya hear me Marie Laveau, de rich white ladies done crossed my door. I ain't gonna drink dis beer myself, no. I'm payin' it to you! Like de white peoples come to you, yo' gonna send 'em to Lala. See here? De beer fo' yo.' I'se done payin' yo' off. (Wallace 1940, 3)

The practice of offering libations to the spirits remains an integral practice in New Orleans Voudou today. It is believed that honoring the Ancestors and the spirits will result in their favor and protection. In Lala's case, her libation would ensure continued good business and prosperity.

FIVE FINGUHS COME

All Voudou Queens and conjure women have their specialties, just like any mainstream Western doctor. For Lala, it was working with candles. She was especially proud of her skill in this area. And, apparently, it was not just a lot of hype. On more than one occasion, she demonstrated her adeptness, leaving interviewers scratching their heads as they watched the candle flames dance in response to her questions and songs. Even as the interviewers continued with patterns of dismissive and patronizing attitudes toward her, they could not deny the mysteries on display right in front of their eyes.

And that's the mystery of Voudou. Sometime in the spring of 1939, Lala had the opportunity to demonstrate her skill in the conjure arts. Louis Sobol, a writer for the *San Francisco Examiner,* went to see Lala for help with his girlfriend. Describing her as indifferent, Sobol asked Lala to make the woman love him. To find out whether love was coming to him or not, Lala performed a divination.

Lala had Sobol write his beloved's name on a piece of paper and then write his own name on top of hers, as is common practice in spells of a coercive nature. The petition paper was placed under five candles. Lala lit the candles and instructed Sobol to hold his hands over the flame. Simultaneously, she tapped the table and chanted: "O five finguhs come, come, five finguhs come, come. Da man is gone wid love for his love, O five finguhs come, come."

Then, Lala instructed Sobol to observe the five-fingered flame. "Is dey pointin' to'd you—is dey pointin' to'd me?" He watched as the five-fingered flame pointed away from him, and sadness reportedly overcame the Hoodoo Queen's face.

Unfortunately, Sobol had lied about his presenting issue. There was no woman he desired as he was happily married. Back in the day, white folks often lied to infiltrate the Voudous to get information for their salacious newspaper stories and books. Sobol was no exception to the deception.

Suddenly, Sobol saw the five-fingered flame flickering in his direction. "Look!" he exclaimed. "They're toward me now!"

Lala shook her head and told him, "Dey's not fo' love. Dey's fo' money. You is coming into money."

On his way home, Sobol stopped by the Pelican Club for the weekly public drawing of policy numbers. He chose three numbers: 5, 18, and 35. Twelve numbers were picked by volunteers from the rotating canister. Sure enough, of the twelve numbers selected by the volunteers, three numbers were 5, 18, and 35. Sobol had won forty-five dollars! Lala was right—he came into money!

PAGES FROM LALA'S GRIMOIRE

One of the absolute treasures we have from the Federal Writers' Project (FWP) is a collection of gris gris formulas that Lala provided to the interviewers. After they paid her $1.25, Lala tied three black-cat bones to a mojo bag containing steel dust, Returning Powder, and a piece of horse's hair and gave it to the interviewers. Lala then shared the following workings and gris gris (McKinney 1937, 8–9).

Lucky Garters

Two garters were to be made and worn: one red and one yellow. Red is for victory; yellow is for luck. Each garter had an attached mojo bag containing steel dust, money seed, and essence of verbena. To hold the bag in place, a piece of red elastic was sewn over the garter. Lucky garters were perfect for ladies of the night, gambling women, and any woman in a Cleo May frame of mind. Cleo May is a hoodoo working designed to improve a woman's standard of living by attracting a generous man of means.

To Dress a House

"When a house is crossed or hoodooed, get some wintergreen, jack honey sucker, and perbina essence. Sprinkle this around your house, and it will run the evil spirits away." To dress a house when it is crossed means to restore a home that is cursed or haunted to a place of peace. The ingredients Lala describes are liquids—either oils or essences—of wintergreen, Japanese honeysuckle, and essence of verbena. These would be combined and sprinkled around the home to repel and banish evil and negativity.

To Kill

Lala never hid the fact that she was a two-headed conjure doctor who had mastered the art of harming as well as healing. It comes as no surprise that she would have a working for killing someone. It is equally as unremarkable that she would not give the full disposition of the working to the interviewers, as this remains common practice for many reasons, the least of which is to protect her power and tradition. According to Lala, to kill someone you must "write the target's name five times forward and five times backwards on a piece of paper. Split a red fish in half and put the name in it. Sew it up with black thread."

To Tame a Court

This is Lalas's very brief description of the notorious cow-tongue spell that is popular even today with hoodoo practitioners. "Put names of judge, district attorney, grand jury and witnesses on a calf's tongue then split the tongue in half. It will keep the court from swearing on the accused." Lala's account of this working lacks quite a few details, including the fact that the tongue, which can be purchased from a grocery store, is slit lengthwise and the names are put inside. A variety of ingredients such as red pepper and slippery elm are added. The tongue is then sewn closed with black thread and placed in the freezer or nailed to a tree.

Altar for Marie Laveau (photo courtesy of the author).

Marie Laveau, Voudou Queen of New Orleans

Marie Laveau was a voodooienne. She was the queen of them all. She used to say prayers and mix different things to give people to drink, to rub with, to throw over your shoulder, to throw in the river. Oh! She had a million things to do but everything would happen just like she would say.

—Aileen Eugene, 1930

Today, Marie Laveau's name is nearly synonymous with the term "Voudou Queen." They say she never died and instead transformed into a black crow who soars over the Cities of the Dead. Some say she died after living nearly one hundred years. Pretty much everyone in New Orleans will tell you that she still walks the streets of the French Quarter, haunts the nearby bayous, and grants wishes to pilgrims who knock on her tomb.

In life, she assisted all of the influential politicians of her day. She had tea on the businessmen, lawyers, law enforcement, and the bourgeoisie. She was the premiere spiritual consultant for the city, hands down. Her clients included the queen of England and the emperor of China; each sent her elegant gifts in gratitude for her assistance. Lafayette is said to have kissed her forehead. Yes indeed, Marie Laveau is the most famous of all the Voudou Queens to have ever lived in New Orleans.

Marie Catherine Laveaux was born a free woman of color, a Louisiana Creole, on September 10, 1801. Her great-grandmother, Marguerite, was likely born in Senegal. Marie married a freeman of color who was employed as a carpenter, Jacques Paris. Marie and Jacques had two children together, Felicité and Marie Angèlie Paris, who died in childhood. After Jacques went missing, he was assumed dead, and Marie was referred to as Widow Paris. Recent research by LSU doctoral student Kenetha Harrington, however, has revealed that Jacques moved to Baton Rouge perhaps for work and did not die until 1823. He was reportedly buried without a marker in St. Joseph Catholic cemetery in Baton Rouge.

Later, Marie became the placée of Louis Christophe Dominique Duminy de Glapion, a white man of French nobility. They had seven children together between 1827 and 1838, but only two of their children survived until adulthood. The two daughters, Marie Helöise Euchariste and Marie Philomène, have both been suggested to be Marie Laveau II, stepping into their mother's shoes as Voudou Queen upon her death. This gave the illusion of Marie Laveau having lived an extraordinarily long life.

Since Marie Helöise died in 1862, and her mother lived until 1881, there is no way she could have succeeded her. Marie Philomène, on the other hand, lived beyond her mother's death until 1897. Known as Madame Legendre, she was a devout Catholic like her mother. Still, according to some early interviews by the Louisiana Writers' Project, she had no interest in Voudou. Others indicated that she was involved in spiritual work, but it was much more on the downlow.

For example, she was reported by a woman named Martha Grey to "make novenas for those in trouble, like the Spiritualists do today. She had an altar with red lamps" (Michinard 1941). Furthermore, Marie Philomène lived with her mother, and they were reportedly very close. Growing up in the home of a Voudou Queen indicates that, in all likelihood, she was exposed to the religion at least, if not initiated in it (Alvarado 2020).

While most famous for her role as Voudou Queen of New Orleans, Marie Laveau is most beloved by those in the city for her charitable works. As a devout Catholic, she observed and practiced the Corporal Works of Mercy. The Seven Works of Mercy are: feed the hungry, give drink to the thirsty, shelter the homeless, visit the sick, visit the prisoners, bury the dead, and give alms to the poor. When her life is explored, it is clear Marie practiced the Works of Mercy every day, whether it was by sheltering runaway slaves and Choctaw market women, ministering to prisoners on death row, or nursing those afflicted with the Saffron Scourge.

Marie Laveau lived during the yellow fever epidemic that lasted for sixty-seven summers in the 19th century and worked tirelessly to comfort and heal the sick. She is well known for her work beside Père Antoine as what we would now call an "essential worker," a nurse. You see, part of her renown in New Orleans is her reputation for healing the sick. She tended to so many sick people, yet still lived to be eighty-one years old. That is quite remarkable, as the average life expectancy for women of color in the 1800s was their twenties. Her longevity fueled the Marie Laveau II legend.

There are a couple of good books available with biographical information about Marie Laveau. My book, *The Magic of Marie Laveau: Embracing the Spiritual Legacy of the Voodoo Queen of New Orleans*, is the latest publication. Instead of repeating what I and others have written elsewhere, I want to share some stories that haven't gotten as much exposure. As a scholar-practitioner from New Orleans, different things catch my eye than other researchers looking at the same material might see. Interpretation and context are everything when sharing cultural information.

While charity work is well within the norms of the Catholic Church, Marie Laveau was known for some peculiarities. For example, Marie Dede, a midwife interviewed by the Federal Writers' Project (FWP) in the late 1930s, reported that every year on All Saints Day, Marie Laveau took a big black box to the graveyard and placed it on an old tomb in the old St. Louis Cemetery. She sat in complete silence on that black box on top of the tomb all day long until the sun went down, at which time she went home (Dillon, Folder 025, 145). No one knows why Marie Laveau did this.

My guess is she was communing with the Ancestors. She may have been sitting on the tomb of a known conjure worker or Voudou Queen who had preceded her and sought to amplify her own power and perhaps make a contract with the spirit. Or maybe it was the gravesite of one or more of her children who did not survive, which would make sense given she did this on All Saints Day. As a mother, I cannot imagine what it must have been like for her to lose so many children. The grief had to be unbearable. Having a defined time and space to be alone, to grieve, and to commune with them would be highly therapeutic.

Spending time at cemeteries is not unusual for Voudou Queens and hoodoos. You would be surprised at the kind of magickal things done in graveyards. Court case work, for example, is prevalent, in part because Baron Samedi and Manman Brigit reside there, and they are the Voudou spirits of judgment and justice. Marie Laveau was known for doing court case work in St. Roch cemetery. She did love spells there, too.

In New Orleans Voudou and hoodoo, the standard offering to the Dead is fifteen cents. Fifteen cents is left at the cemetery gates as the price of admission, and fifteen cents is left at any grave where conjuring is done. Note that this may not be the complete offering provided to the spirits, but it is considered the standard minimum. Now, Marie Laveau is reported as having a strange habit of adding a fifteen-cent surcharge on top of any price she charged. None of the informants reporting this, however, could explain why. According to FWP informant Joe Landry:

> She knew you were going to git out. When you were done you go back to her and the charge may be $10.15, bad case $20.15, maybe $50.15, for very bad case, but always the fifteen cents was added. She never explained why. (Posey 1939)

Apparently, Marie Laveau magickally targeted judge, jury, and witnesses, and her price was set according to the complexity of the case. I would guess that she added the fifteen cents as payment to the Ancestors, acknowledging their importance in the Laveau lineage.

Marie Laveau was famously known for her Voudou dances and activities in Congo Square. Another person who knew her, Raymond Riveros, said she used to go to Congo Square at least three to four times a week. She brought her black snake with her in a box, put the serpent by the fountain, and danced awhile. Then, without speaking a word to anyone, she placed the snake back in the box and left just as smoothly as she had arrived.

Some people complained to the authorities about the Voudou Queen and her scary snake, so two policemen were stationed at each of the four gates. When Marie approached the entrance to the square, she just looked at them and proceeded to walk right on in. No one ever tried to stop her, and no one ever tried to harm her. She was the Boss Woman in every sense of the word.

If you aren't from New Orleans, you might wonder why a Voudou Queen is so famous. It is true that we have the media and the tourist industry to thank for many persistent legends of a nefarious nature. But, Marie Laveau was a real woman who accomplished extraordinary feats in her lifetime. If we think about the sociopolitical climate of the times in which she lived, it helps us understand just how unique she was. People loved her, and people feared her. Mostly though, she was respected.

Whenever we talk about where Marie Laveau learned her Voudou, it all comes down to guesswork, really. I mean, we can assume her mother knew and practiced and taught her, as has been suggested, but we also hear of her learning from some Voudou priestesses before her. In addition, part of the Laveau legend says that she worked alongside Doctor John Montenée, a popular gris gris man in New Orleans at the time. However, it is interesting that there are no known documented instances of Marie

Laveau and Doctor John working together for Voudou or business or anything else, for that matter.

I did find one notice in a newspaper from April 26, 1855, from the treasurer's office, where each was listed as operating an establishment or activity without a license. Looking at the very tiny print, it appears that they were both at the same place: Bayou St. John, at the lake. Could it be they were both at one of the famous Voudou ceremonies held there? On the other hand, Marie Laveau is listed as operating a grocery and liquor store while Jean Labeau (one of the alternate names for Doctor John) is listed as running a café house.

In *The Magic of Marie Laveau*, I documented a distinct religio-magickal tradition I called Laveau Voudou. In that book, I also identified Marie Laveau's spiritual court—that is, those spirits that she likely served—based on oral history, newspaper accounts, interviews with people who knew her, and other historical accounts. I found references to St. Peter, St. Anthony, St. John the Baptist, St. Michael, Mami Wata, St. Maroon, Li Grand Zombi, Damballah Wedo, and the Spirit of Death. Recently, I came across additional evidence of the presence of Mami Wata in New Orleans from writings published by an anonymous author in 1750 in *L'Essai sur l'Esclavage at Observations sur l'Etat Present des Colonies*, cited in an article by George Simpson (1945):

> The dance called at Surinam *Watur mama,* and in our colonies "the water mother," is strictly forbidden to them. They make a great mystery of it, and all that is known of it is that it excites very much their imagination.

In 1750, it would very much have been against the law for slaves to practice their African traditions; hence the reference that it "is strictly forbidden to them." It is noteworthy that Marie Laveau had many rituals at the water's edge. Whether it was a bayou, the Mississippi River, Lake Pontchartrain, or some minor tributary leading into the swamp, the element of water figures prominently in Marie Laveau's rituals. Though she was not born until 1801, the reference to a water mother sets the precedence for Mami Wata's existence in New Orleans much earlier than previously believed.

In 1820, the *Louisiana Gazette* reported a police raid on a Faubourg Tremé home in New Orleans where ritual objects, including a fetish of a woman with the lower extremities of a snake, were confiscated. That is a depiction of the water goddess of African origin, Mami Wata.

I have also suggested that Marie Laveau worked with the Spirit of Death, Baron Samedi or Papa Guédé. Initially, I came to this conclusion after reading that Marie Laveau called upon the Spirit of Death in a ceremony "when suddenly, there appeared in the group the Voudoo, being clad in the garb of death . . . he wore a skull and crossbones upon his bosom and carried a scythe in one hand and a small wooden coffin in the other" (*Times Daily Picayune* 1890, 10). Reportedly, the Spirit of Death knelt in front of the serpent and knocked on the ground three times. Grabbing a rag doll from the altar, he placed it into the coffin along with a handful of dirt gathered from the ground—more than likely grave dirt. Once he closed the coffin, it signaled the point of the ceremony when all of the participants should approach the gris gris pot and receive their portion. The Dance of Death, known today as the Banda, commenced (Alvarado 2020).

Another clue recently became evident. According to one individual who called himself Pops, "This was around 1875. She was dressed in a long purple robe with some kind of rope around her waist . . . da women coworkers wore purple, too. Da men wore white and purple . . ." (Dillon, Folder 025). Voudous who serve the Guédé and Baron Samedi wear purple when conducting rituals specifically for those spirits, as purple, black, and white are their colors. This informant was about eighty-one years old at the time of the interview and was believed to have been a reliable witness and suspected of knowing much more than he offered to interviewers.

Calling upon Baron Samedi for making magick is consistent with what we know about him and his role in Voudou. He is associated with a type of death conjure called *l'envoi morts*, or *Expéditions*, meaning "Sending of the Dead" (Métraux 1959). Expeditions are a type of death conjure that, when performed, resemble the Marie Laveau ceremony.

Marie Laveau was buried in St. Louis Cemetery No. 1, according to the archdiocese records. However, this fact remains hotly contested by locals who insist that her body was moved at some point by relatives and reinterred elsewhere. If so, there are no records to indicate that it happened as part of a formal process. Some say her spirit would not stay in her tomb, which caused everyone to be so scared, they avoided the cemetery altogether. Some say she still wanders the graveyard in the form of a big, black Newfoundland dog. That's part of the legend. There are no known facts to support that her body was ever moved.

New Orleans Voudou is a living tradition connected by her sacred geography. To devotees, the tomb of the mother of New Orleans Voudou is at its core. It is the second most visited gravesite in the United States, next to Elvis Presley. Tourists and Voudou devotees travel to St. Louis Cemetery No. 1 to pay their respects and make a wish on her famous tomb. Three cross marks (XXX) are made with the finger while making the wish and imploring the Voudou Queen to answer. People used to use pieces of broken red brick from neighboring graves to draw their cross marks directly onto her tomb. New regulations have been implemented since the restoration of her tomb in 2014, and the practice is no longer allowed.

The new rules also prevent people from visiting her tomb by themselves, and you must now be accompanied by a tour guide. Needless to say, this created a need for a public alternative, and Mambo Sallie Ann Glassman of La Source Ancienne Ounfo heeded the call. A new shrine was erected in the New Orleans Healing Center on St. Claude Avenue. Just inside the lobby is the International Shrine of Marie Laveau. People light candles and leave little slips of paper with their wishes written on them at the shrine. The shrine was formally installed during a blessing ceremony at the Sacred Music Festival in March 2015.

Éliphas Lévi, 1854, Baphomet, also known as the Sabbatic Goat, from *Dogme et Rituel de la Haute Magie*. The image appears in Toups' *Magick High and Low* as the God of the Witches.

12

Mary Oneida Toups, Witch Queen of New Orleans

I am High Priestess of the Religious Order of Witchcraft and High Priestess of the Parent Coven. I am an acknowledged, recognized, and practicing witch!

—MARY ONEIDA TOUPS

New Orleans is well known for its Voudous and Voudou activity. There is a whole segment of the tourist trade devoted to Voudou—Voodoo-themed stores, Voodoo potato chips, Voodoo beer, and Voodoo tours, to name but a few. Not so well known but equally as present are the witches of New Orleans. Old New Orleans Traditional Witchcraft, as I came to know it, was not as well known as Voudou in the city—until the TV show *American Horror Story: Coven,* that is.

If you are a local and in tune with the supernatural calling cards of the Crescent City, you may have caught the one line uttered by Fiona Goode, high priestess and supreme witch, in *American Horror Story*'s third season. In that episode, Fiona Goode, played by Jessica Lange, and members of her New Orleans coven were on their way to Popp's Fountain. "Back in the seventies," said Fiona, "Mary Oneida Toups led an alternative coven down here." This one line piqued the curiosity of a whole new generation of witches who had never heard of Oneida before.

Back in the day, Popp's Fountain was overgrown, unkempt, and neglected. But the beauty of the purple wisteria, pink azaleas, and oak trees around the legendary magickal space was seen by earth-loving women and men as lush, fertile grounds. With its fabulous, classical-Greek architectural style and a stage conducive to high magick rituals, Popp's Fountain on Lake Pontchartrain was the perfect place for Mary Oneida Toups's coven of witches to celebrate the Sabbats, commune with the spirits, or sit in quiet solitude. I've been there many times and can vouch for it firsthand.

Close up of the Popp's Fountain Complex. You can see how conducive such a space would be for high or low ceremonial magick. This image was taken or made as part of a Works Progress Administration employee's official duties. (As a work of the U.S. federal government, the image is in the public domain [17 U.S. Codes § 101 and § 105].)

Mary Oneida Toups is considered the official Witch Queen of New Orleans in the 20th century. Known simply as Oneida, she was born on April 25, 1925, to Arthur Hodgin and Mary Ellen Killing of Meridian, Mississippi. Founder of the Religious Order of Witchcraft in New Orleans, her church was formally incorporated by the secretary of state on February 1, 1972. It was the first church of witchcraft to be recognized as such in the state of Louisiana. Oneida reported that there were more than fifty members in her local coven (*Hattiesburg American* 1978).

Oneida lived a normal life in Mississippi as a wife and mother up until 1969 or so. We don't know a lot about her early life, but according to folklorist Alyne Pustanio, "Like many youths of her generation, when she reached her teens, she began to feel restless and took to the road. Hitchhiking, exploring the back roads and byways of the rural South, her path eventually brought her to New Orleans, where she soon became part of a burgeoning bohemian movement already thriving there" (Pustanio 2013, 65).

The local supernatural environment in New Orleans had been developing through the social storms of the sixties. Feminism, civil rights, and the sexual revolution coincided with drug use, music, and the Age of Aquarius. The installment of Catholic mysticism and folk sacramentals had been firmly in place since the 1800s. Voudou, ever present, remained underground. The city was primed and ready to receive a new witch to behold.

Oneida arrived in New Orleans in 1970 and would soon meet her future husband, Boots Toups. They shared a close group of friends that included the late Mac Rebennack, also known as Dr. John, the famous New Orleans musician who took the moniker of the legendary gris gris man of the 19th century, Doctor John Montenée. This group of friends would become some of Oneida's most loyal followers. Together, they formed the core of the coven she would create with Boots. Oneida referred to this close circle of friends as her "Scribes" (Pustanio 2013, 65).

Oneida presumably dove headfirst into her studies of the occult arts when she got to New Orleans. One of the remarkable things about her was how quickly she became adept in magick. With no known background in magick before coming to New Orleans, she mainly learned by reading popular occult books, grimoires, and religious texts.

Katina Smith, who became high priestess of the Religious Order of Witchcraft after Hurricane Katrina, stated that Oneida might have studied via correspondence course under occultist Israel Regardie (1907–1985) and learned from local New Orleans witches (personal communication,

July 2019). Israel Regardie was a well-known British author and ceremonial magician who was once the acting secretary to Aleister Crowley. Regardie was a member of the Hermetic Order of the Golden Dawn and wrote fifteen books on occultism.

Like Marie Laveau, Oneida was business savvy. Her shop, the Witches' Workshop—or what I always called the "witchcraft shop"—was the first place I bought a dressed candle and learned about anointing candles for ritual use. When I was a young girl of five or six, I was introduced to spirit communication and candle magick by one of the women in my family. She taught me about basic magick (what Oneida called low magick), communicating with the spirits, and conducting séances, all with the aid of a single white candle. She didn't put anything on the candles—that I knew of, in any event—and just used a simple household candle or taper candle. So, I was familiar with candles and magick. But I had never seen one anointed in magickal oils and herbs like these. I fell in love with them the moment I laid eyes on them. I loved how they smelled. I thirsted for the energy they exuded.

Oneida loved her candles, too. She insisted that candles must be in solid colors to create the proper vibrations for rituals. Of them, she said, "Candle rituals are amazingly successful. This is considered low magick and does not require a vast amount of knowledge of the occult. It is assured that failure only occurs when a person uses a candle with false faith and does not perfect the ritual" (Spraker 1973, 16).

As a teenager, I loved venturing into the French Quarter and visiting the witchcraft shop. It smelled so mysterious. Thick wafts of aromatic incense burning in the air permeated the psyches of all who entered there. The lights were dim, adding to the ambiance. Adorning the shelves were the usual potions and notions you might find in other Voudou shops in the French Quarter—magickal oils, animal parts, occult books, and figural candles.

The most popular curio in the store at the time was the dried bats. Bat hearts were especially desirable. "It's important to sell people the whole dried bat so they can be confident it's the real thing and not just an old chicken heart," Oneida said. She explained that dried bat hearts are coveted by "gamblers who often carry them on trips to Las Vegas" (Sutton 1972, 25). Even a black cat named Voodoo took up residence there. There was a pure white cat, too, although I don't know what its name was. Apparently, both cats were said to be Oneida's familiars.

I was always interested in witchcraft, the occult, and the mysteries held by those traditions. For some reason, I felt drawn to Oneida's shop and the activities there. This shop was one of those places that just represented the craft so well in the 1970s. When I entered the shop, the woman behind the counter greeted me with a phrase that I sadly cannot remember. Oh, what I would give to be able to retrieve that memory! At the time, I believed it was a greeting of a secret society, not something the everyday person would have known. I keep hoping that I will be reading an old grimoire one day and happen upon that phrase so that I can finally lay that longing to remember to rest.

Oneida was very friendly to me, as she was known to be to all of her customers, though we didn't know each other outside the shop. I was only about fourteen when I discovered her, so there was a definite age difference. In fact, she was the same age as my mother! Still, her shop and the items she sold were made available to me. She was known for taking time out to help new witches and to dispense advice.

I kept that first candle I bought from the witchcraft shop for quite some time before I actually burned it in a ritual. I believed that once I burned the candle, the energy from it would dissipate, and somehow, I would lose what I was holding on to. There was some real power in that candle. Today, I still fix my candles like the high priestess of the Religious Order of Witchcraft, Mary Oneida Toups, taught me. It is a tiny part of her legacy and lineage that I am blessed to have and to hold as someone who is not a member of the Order.

I was too young to join her coven then, or I would have, more than likely. Even with her paid membership–driven coven, where you could pay a hundred dollars a year to join, she required folks to be at least twenty-one years old. Instead, I initiated into transcendental meditation at the Hare Krishna temple in New Orleans. What can I say? I was searching, and the Hare Krishnas didn't have an age requirement. And the Beatles were all up into it, too.

Like Voudou in New Orleans, witchcraft has the flavor of gumbo. Different covens have different ways of doing things. Factor in the number of solitary witches—those who do not belong to a coven and instead practice on their own—and you have many different expressions of witchcraft. Oneida's church was concerned with godliness: "My religion is witchcraft. It's important to me. If you cannot respect it, leave."

In 1975, Oneida published her first and only book, *Magick, High and Low*. It received high praise from the likes of Israel Regardie. The book is piecemealed together mainly from public domain grimoires and magickal texts by Wallace Budge, Éliphas Lévi, and Heinrich Cornelius Agrippa. It includes chapters on the basics of high and low magick, tarot cards and their meanings, images of several Egyptian deities, discussions about the Tree of Life, astrology, and more. Oneida's husband, Boots, wrote the introduction for the book. The book has long been out of print, and if you can find a copy, be prepared to pay several hundred dollars for it as an occult collectible.

Little is known about Oneida's Religious Order of Witchcraft. In a couple of interviews, she explained the meanings behind some occult symbols and practices. Her practice included high magick (ceremonial magick) and low magick (folk magick, spellcraft) and the study of sacred texts such as the Bible, Talmud, and Koran. "Our religion is very old and combines elements of various philosophies, as most religions. Mainly, it's based on old Egyptian beliefs and includes elements of the Kabbalah . . . Free Masonry and Rosicrucianism, among others" (*Hattiesburg American* 1978, 7).

Contrary to the usual stereotypes of naked women dancing around boiling cauldrons, Oneida described her coven as conservative, refusing to admit long-haired hippie types, druggies, or anyone with a police record. "Ours is a true religion," she said. "We don't run around in the nude." Among witches, powers include invoking spirits and "reordering physical phenomena like transporting an object through a wall—depending on each witch's level of preparation and study" (*Daily World* 1972, 3).

According to Oneida, her coven celebrated four major and four minor sabbats a year. All Hallow's Eve is, not surprisingly, one of them. In an interview in 1978 with the *Hattiesburg American,* she shared an All Hallow's Eve ritual:

> The actual ceremony is very simple. We will have an altar, which holds, among other articles, an "athame," a knife with which I will draw a holy protective circle, a chalice, a cross, candles, and a red rose symbolizing love and life. We break bread, eat salt and drink wine, established rituals of Catholicism, which are also part of our religion. After the ceremony, we have a simple party to celebrate this holiday. That's all there is to it. It's very innocent but also very meaningful. (*Hattiesburg American* 1978)

Oneida provided information about basic candle magick. She used the *Master Book of Candle Burning* by Henri Gamache as a reference book. She also used the Book of Psalms, which is quite unusual in the case of typical witchcraft. However, in the context of New Orleans, with the strong influence of the Catholic Church and Voudou on the spiritual traditions there, it really isn't all that surprising. I took the liberty of organizing some of the information about Oneida's candle magick into a handy chart on page 138 for my witchy readers (see Table 1).

Table 1. Oneida's Witchcraft Candle Chart

CANDLE COLOR	PURPOSE	ZODIAC SIGN	PSALM
Black	Confusion, discord, evil, loss	Libra	55, 109
Blue	Grace, love, mercy, subduing an enemy	Aquarius	28, 32
Brown	Uncertainty, neutrality	Scorpio	73, 83
Gold	Attraction, persuasion, charm	Virgo/Sagittarius	47
Grey	Cancellation, misfortune, protection	Unknown	22
Green	Fertility, finance, luck	Cancer	62, 11
Lime	Anger, discord, jealousy	Unknown	55
Orange	Adaptability, encourage-ment, peace of mind	Unknown	37
Pink	Success, honor	Unknown	65
Purple	Ambition, commanding, compelling, power	Unknown	130
Red	Love, strength	Capricorn/Gemini/Leo/Taurus	138
White	Purity, sincerity, truth	Aries	129
Yellow	Dispel evil	Unknown	144

Like the celebrated Voudou Queen of New Orleans, Marie Laveau, Oneida held ceremonies on the shores of Lake Pontchartrain. She also held a city permit to conduct rituals in City Park, famously at Popp's Fountain. In fact, Popp's Fountain was a favorite gathering spot for her coven. It was secluded and overgrown, making it ideal for covert ritual activity. Since its initial construction in 1937, however, Popp's Fountain has undergone significant restoration. A new venue called the Arbor Room was added for parties and wedding receptions, and the surrounding twelve acres of land is now fenced in.

Like other points of occult interest in New Orleans, visitors report having strange experiences when visiting the fountain. Time seems to stand still, for example, whereby people will spend hours at the fountain but feel as though only a few minutes have passed. I remember feeling that myself when I was there. It is quite a surreal experience.

But back to Oneida. Around the same time her book was published, her marriage to Boots came to an end. In addition, her lease to the Witches' Workshop was up. She decided to relocate and reopen in a different location. According to New Orleans folklorist Alyne Pustanio, sources who helped with the move said a man showed up with a going-away present, "a hat box with something rolling around inside. When Oneida opened the box, she was shocked to find a fully intact preserved human head; thinking it a prop of some kind, she showed it to her friends and even pretended to chase them around with it" (2013, 70).

Apparently, she left it behind rather than take it with her when she moved, a decision that landed her in the newspapers and fueled rumors of human sacrifice:

> A mummified head found in the refuse of an abandoned occult shop in New Orleans probably was a study tool for medical students before becoming a possession of a self-proclaimed witch, a pathologist said Tuesday. Dr. Monroe Samuels said there was no reason to suspect foul play in the man's death. The head was discovered Sunday by a woman cleaning trash from a building previously occupied by Oneida Toups. Mrs. Toups said she was a practitioner of Egyptian magic and a witch and that the head was a gift from some friends. She said she threw it away because of bad "vibrations." (*Calgary Herald* 1977, 15)

Now, having human skulls and bones used to be part and parcel for witchcraft and Voudou in New Orleans, and still is, truth be told. But it's not advertised, that's for sure. Mummified heads? Not so much unless you have a shop in New Orleans; then it is tourism currency. What strikes me about the mummified head incident is how unusual it would be to leave it in a box and hope someone else disposes of it. Nevertheless, that's precisely what Oneida said she did. She felt some funky energy from it and just abandoned it! She wrapped it in a cloth, put it back in the hatbox, and left it at her shop when she moved. She said she hoped that the new tenant would simply throw out the box without looking in it. But think about it; people are curious. Most would look in a box left at an occult shop to see what might be inside. Lawsy, I'm sure you wouldn't expect to find a mummified head, though!

Predictably, the new tenant did indeed open the box and find the mummified head, which more than likely scared the living daylights out of her. She subsequently called the police, which resulted in an examination by the coroner, Dr. Monroe Samuels. After Dr. Samuels examined the head, he determined it was the head of a black man. Because it had sharp cuts on the side of the head, the coroner believed it was likely the property of a medical or dental school previously. Weird.

Oneida said, "It's supposed to be an African prince. I intended to put it in a glass case and display it at my shop, but it started giving me bad luck. I didn't like the vibrations" (*Crowley Post-Signal* 1977, 2).

Now, there's more tea to this story, and it's quite tasty.

Interestingly, Dr. John, the famous New Orleans musician, bought a mummified head to use as a prop from a trapper in Georgia who "sold pelts and snakeskins and the like" (Rebennack and Rummel 1994, 168). He called him "Prince," dressed him up as an extra musician, sat him behind the keyboard, and no one was the wiser.

As Dr. John tells it in his book, *Under a Hoodoo Moon*, he and some gris gris people got into trouble when the Santeria Temple of Baal was busted. Prince was confiscated by the police. The man who ran the Santeria Temple, Jack, was running guns under the guise of religious artifacts, and Prince was among the artifacts. From there, Prince ended up in the hands of the coroner Dr. Minyard. The police believed the head belonged to a murder victim, but Dr. Minyard traced his "fancy dental work and discovered he had been used as a practice patient in a dental school in the 1800s. A century and many adventures later, Prince now resides in Charity Hospital, along with a host of other medical oddities" (Rebennack and Rummel 1994, 168).

Dr. John says all this took place while his album *In the Right Place* was hitting the charts, which would make it 1973, when the album was released. Could this be the same mummified head that Oneida had come to dispossess in 1977? Dr. John called it "Prince," and Oneida called it an African prince. It would not be a stretch at all, as they moved in the same circles. Boots and Dr. John were good friends and started the Temple of Voodoo together, which they operated out of one of Oneida's shops.

As an aside, I wonder where Prince is today. Charity Hospital is no more; Hurricane Katrina did an excellent job of cleaning her out. Despite being sanitized and ready for business after the storm, the city decided to keep the doors closed and build a new hospital. Did anyone try to preserve the medical oddities that were in Charity Hospital? I do not know. If so, I'm sure it wasn't the kind of thing that would be a priority during a disaster like Hurricane Katrina. But who knows, someone may have preserved some of them, and maybe Prince is still out there somewhere in someone's private collection.

Sadly, in 1980, Oneida's life took a turn for the worse when she received a terminal cancer diagnosis.

> Around this time, she moved in with a close friend who offered to care for her during her illness. A certain individual in New Orleans these days likes to take credit as the woman who nursed Oneida Toups, but in reality Oneida's nurse was a dear friend named Carol, a woman she had known since her earliest days in New Orleans. As Oneida's health declined, Carol remained staunchly at her side. Then in September 1981 Oneida, the one and only Witch Queen of New Orleans, succumbed to her illness and died. (Pustanio 2013, 70)

Oddly enough, Dr. John says that Oneida died from being poisoned by another witch in the city. According to Lady Katina, Oneida died of a brain lesion in September 1981. There is no public record of her death, and her death certificate remains under seal in Louisiana. There is no record of her husband's death either, and their burial sites, if any, have not been made public. Dr. John mentioned that Boots had disappeared, but he didn't know if Boots had died or not and dared not ask those who reportedly saw him around the city. He said after Oneida died, "Boots got shot a couple more times and got poisoned! At last, I heard he died, although I never knew for sure if this was true" (Rebeneck and Rummel 1994, 170).

It seems as if they were both forgotten, or their burials were intentionally hidden. Attempts to locate Oneida's burial site have not been successful. The general public and members of the Religious Order of Witchcraft reportedly do not know to this day what happened to Oneida's remains. It is possible she was never buried, and her urn is in the possession of an appointed caretaker. One informant mentioned that Oneida's daughter has her urn, but another source reports that the urn is in their possession.

After Oneida's death, leadership for the Religious Order of Witchcraft and her shop were taken over by Oneida's colleague and coven member, Russell George, a high priest in the Order. He ultimately operated his own business there called the Witches Closet (Fensterstock 2018). He remained active in the craft and passed on Oneida's teachings until he died in 2014.

After Hurricane Katrina, leadership was assumed by the aforementioned Lady Katina Smith, who served for approximately fifteen years. In 2017, she stepped down as high priestess and handed over the crown to Lady Heather Finn in Connecticut. The Religious Order of Witchcraft continues to provide training in the magickal system created by Oneida Toups.

Five years after Oneida's passing, witchcraft and Voudou were "no longer a highly visible local presence" (Bookhardt 1986, 26). Talk of the witch queen turned to whispers. Nonetheless, like so many of the magickal figures of New Orleans, local lore tells of the ghosts of Oneida and Boots still roaming the city. And, like other local ghosts, they sometimes manifest in physical form and have conversations with folks, especially tourists, who do not realize who—or what—they are talking to. When tourists describe their interactions with the spirits to locals, they are surprised to find out they spoke to the spirits of the legendary witch queen and her husband: Oneida and Boots Toups.

There have been many magickal figures in New Orleans, some more iconic than others, but all are legends in their own right. Mary Oneida Toups was legit. Forty-six years ago, I connected with Oneida and her magick on an ethereal level. Her witchcraft shop was a point on the sacred supernatural geography of the city, a connection to the soul of New Orleans, with Oneida reigning supreme. Blessed be.

Papa Legba, by Denise Alvarado.

13

Papa Legba, Gatekeeper and Guardian of the Crossroads

The path of destiny is large, large like a large penis.

—Papa Legba

The notorious legend of the "Black Man at the Crossroads" ignites much curiosity across cultures. References to making deals with devils at dusty four-way crossroads are found as early as the 5th century in the writings of St. Jerome. In the 6th century, we see the legend of Theofilus, who sold his soul to the devil in exchange for a position as bishop. Numerous instructions for conjuring demons exist in the old grimoires.

Of course, we cannot ignore the infamous deal with the devil allegedly made by renowned bluesman Robert Johnson. According to legend, Johnson went to a crossroads at midnight and summoned Satan, who appeared as a large black man. Johnson gave his guitar to him, and the "devil" tuned it, played a few songs, and gave the guitar back. In exchange for Johnson's soul, the devil gave him the skill to play the legendary blues for which he is famous.

But who is that black man at the crossroads? Some say he is Satan. Others say he is Papa Legba, the Voudou spirit everyone nowadays confuses with Baron Samedi, the Voudou Spirit of Death. Still others say it's neither Legba nor Baron Samedi; instead, he is an aspect of Legba called Met Kalfu.

Historically, it was the habit of early missionaries to liken Legba to the Christian devil, whose evil nature must be feared. However, Legba is neither demon nor devil, nor is he Satan. In fact, he is arguably the most important and beloved spirit in the New Orleans Voudou pantheon. He serves as the guardian of the Poto Mitan, the center of power and support in the sacred temples. All ceremonies begin and end with him, and there can be no communication with any of the other spirits without consulting him first. Papa Legba is the cunning celestial trickster, master linguist, warrior, guardian of crossroads and entrances, and destiny's personal messenger.

Papa Legba's gift for linguistics enables him to translate the requests of humans into the languages of the spirits. In Legba's vévé—his ritual symbol—is the crossroads. He is known by several names in New Orleans: Papa Legba, Papa Alegba, Papa Labas, and Papa Limba. During Mardi Gras season, a popular shout by revelers is "A Labas!" This is a reference to St. Peter, who has functioned for more than a hundred years as the Catholic cloak for Legba in New Orleans Voudou.

So, Legba is not the devil or Satan personified, but he is syncretized with some Catholic saints. In Haiti and Cuba, he is syncretized with St. Anthony, St. Lazarus, and sometimes St. Peter. In New Orleans, he is strongly associated with St. Peter and St. Anthony. Wherever he is found, he is the consummate trickster, seamlessly adapting to the environments in which he is found.

LEGBA'S AFRICAN ORIGINS

Papa Legba is found in myriad forms at doorways and crossroads as the African god whose origins are with the Fon people of Dahomey (present-day Benin). He came to the Americas with the African Diaspora and has a prominent and essential place in New Orleans Voudou.

According to one legend, Papa Legba is the youngest son of Mawu and Liza, the creators of the world. Mawu and Liza are portrayed as twins but are one in spirit. Mawu is the female aspect associated with the east, the night moon, fertility, motherhood, and night. Liza is the male aspect associated with the west, the daytime sun, heat, work, and strength. In another legend, Legba is the son of Oshun, the orisha of divinity, femininity, fertility, beauty, and love.

In West African Vodun culture, every household and even every person in the household can have a shrine to Legba. This consists of an open pot set upon a mound of earth. Sacrifices of palm oil, cornmeal, entrails of chickens, or larger animals are placed in the pot if demanded by Fa. Fa is destiny, the Fon system of divination. Dogs are sacred to Legba, and it is considered a positive sign from Legba when a dog eats the offerings from his pot and shrine.

In American society, we see Legba as the Black Man at the crossroads or as the media-fabricated Black Man in the cemetery with a top hat and cane. However, in West Africa, he is depicted as male and female, sometimes as a healer, and sometimes as a protector. In one form, he is shown as an "apologetic Legba," petitioned for forgiveness when a person has insulted the gods through awful behaviors like rape and burglary. In another form, he is depicted as a mound of dirt. And this might surprise some Westerners; sometimes, Legba is depicted as a fertility god with a huge, erect penis. In one Fon tale, for example, the god of divination and fate, Fa,

> sneaks into Legba's home and sleeps with his wife. Legba asks her why and she says that his penis wasn't big enough for her. Challenged, Legba eats an enormous amount of food and swears to have sex with her until she tires, all the while calling out "the path of destiny is large, large like a large penis." Legba then made Fa stay in the house, while Legba takes his wife and hits the road, vowing that he will always be first, and will always be ready to fuck. (Davis 1991)

Sexual virility is not the only thing Legba is known for. Dahomean (Fon) cosmology tells us that Legba was the first of the gods to make *gbo*, as it was gifted to him by the forest spirits called Azizzas. The Azizzas are small monkey-like creatures who sometimes live in ant beds and termite mounds and make themselves known to hunters. Gbo is the original system of magick that informs how to construct and use charms that address the everyday conditions of life, much like our American hoodoo and root-work. The Azizzas taught Legba the original mysteries of the leaves and the proper formula for constructing gbo, including combining ingredients and observing taboos.

Back in the day, when the gods were hungry and before the people fed them, Legba was up to his usual shenanigans. This time, he created gbo in the form of a snake and placed it in the middle of the road lead-ing to the market so that passersby would encounter it. He instructed the snake to bite everyone who walked by, which it did. When a person was bitten, Legba would run up to them and ask for an offering in exchange for a cure. Once he was paid, however, he would run to the market and get his fill of his favorite drink, akasan, along with palm oil and water and partake of everything himself.

One day, a man stopped and pointed at the snake and asked Legba, "What is this thing in the road that bites people?"

Legba replied, "It is a gbo. Bring me two chickens, eighty cowries and some straw and I will make a gbo for you."

When the man returned with the requested offerings, Legba instructed him on making gbo. He told the man to throw a vine on the ground, which he did, and it promptly turned into a poisonous snake and started biting people. This time, Legba also gave the man the curing gbo, the medicine needed to cure snake bites. The man's name was Awe; thus, Awe is the first human to receive gbo (Blier 1996).

Akasan, Legba's Corn Drink

Ingredients

- 5 cups water, divided
- 2 cinnamon sticks
- 4 to 6 anise stars
- 1 cup of very fine corn flour
- Pinch of salt
- 1 teaspoon of vanilla extract
- 2 (12-ounce) cans of evaporated milk
- Sweeten to taste with brown or white sugar

Directions

Boil 4 cups of water with the cinnamon, salt, and star anise. Combine corn flour, 1 cup of cold water, salt and mix well. Reduce the boiling water to a simmer. Slowly pour the corn-water mixture into the boiling water, stirring constantly, until the drink becomes thick and homogeneous. Allow no more than 5 minutes for this procedure. Add the vanilla extract and 1 can of evaporated milk. Allow to cool completely. Refrigerate to keep cold. Add sugar and milk to taste and remove the cinnamon sticks and star anise prior to consuming. (Chery 2012)

All of the African gods need gbo to be able to cure. It is Legba, however, who knows more about gbo than any other god, which gives him the distinct advantage of curing or causing disorder. And while Legba continues to be the first spirit to be called upon in Voudou rituals, the reason that this is done is not commonly known. The most common understanding for petitioning Legba first is because he is the gatekeeper to the spirit world. As such, he allows or denies the other spirits to come through to help humans when they are called upon.

Beyond this reason, however, is the Fon belief that Legba is acknowledged first because he knows more gbo than any other spiritual or physical being. Thus, calling on him first is to demonstrate honor and respect for his position as the ultimate conjure doctor.

LEGBA IN AMERICAN HORROR STORY: COVEN

Alas, it's not the traditional African stories and depictions that catapulted Papa Legba to the forefront of mainstream American society. Rather, it was *American Horror Story: Coven* that succeeded in doing that. And, as is usually the case with the entertainment industry and African-derived traditions, that did not happen without causing some confusion.

The manner in which Papa Legba was depicted in *American Horror Story: Coven* was a hot mess, to put it bluntly. To begin with, his image was fashioned after the Voudou Spirit of Death, Baron Samedi. In this depiction, he would have been more correctly identified as Met Kalfu, also spelled Mait Carrefour, instead of Papa Legba.

In Haitian Vodou and New Orleans Voudou, Legba has two primary aspects identified by nations and rites: Rada and Petro. The nations correlate to the geographical region from which the spirits originate. For example, the Rada spirits are those originating in Africa, specifically the Kingdom of Dahomey, which is present day Nigeria, Benin, and Togo. As a general rule, the Rada spirits are sweet and cool in nature. Papa Legba is a Rada spirit.

On the other hand, the Petro spirits originate in the New World (Creole and Haitian-born). These spirits are considered hot and bitter with violent tendencies. In New Orleans, Petro spirits are referred to as Flambeaux due to their aggressive, fiery nature. Legba's Petro aspect is called Kafou or Carrefour, meaning the crossroads. He is the lord of black magick and is associated with Guédé and Baron Samedi. This is likely where *American Horror Story* pulled their imagery from.

The Papa Legba character in *American Horror Story: Coven* was given a healthy dose of racial stereotypes. He is shown dressed like a pimp with a penchant for cocaine. In actuality, Legba does not do drugs or wear a top hat, for that matter. You are more likely to find Legba wearing a modest straw hat and smoking a corncob pipe. However, he is the master of gbo and will have calabash gourd filled with his magickal, medicinal powders. But these powders are not designed to be mind-altering substances for recreational use. They are powders that will either harm or cure, cause harmony or discord, and improve or worsen a condition. The powders may work on a purely magickal, supernatural level, or they may have a physical effect. According to Fon Diviner Ayido, as cited in *African Vodun: Art, Psychology and Power:*

> When Legba is dancing he opens a piece of his hat and takes the powder and blows it. Even if he does not say anything, that which he said on the powder previously will begin to happen. If offerings are made and Legba eats well, he will blow white powder and things will work well for you; or he can blow the red powder and negative powers will return to the one who sent it. (Blier 1996, 92)

In addition to his depiction as a drugged-out pimp, *American Horror Story*'s Legba is a sinister spirit who delights in the pain and suffering of others and takes souls before their time. The real Legba does not delight in the suffering of humans, nor does he have dominion over souls. Knowing there were actual New Orleans Voudou practitioners and a cultural consultant on set, the fact that Papa Legba was so incorrectly portrayed is inexcusable.

On the other hand, Papa Legba is commonly depicted in Voudou iconography as an old black man who wears a straw hat, smokes a corn cob pipe, and sports a crooked cane. He can also take the form of a young child fascinated with toys or a strong young man who can guide the way. He is associated with keys, not skulls, and is likened to St. Peter of Catholicism. Just as St. Peter holds the keys to the gates of Heaven, Papa Legba holds the keys to the world of the Invisibles. He likes rum and coffee, not cocaine. He is among the first to be called in Voudou ceremonies because he opens the roads through which the other Voudou spirits (loas) must travel to communicate and interact with humans.

Most importantly, there is no devil in Voudou like there is in Christianity. True, there are spirits with less than stellar attributes in the Voudou pantheon. Still, there is no Satan with legions of demons under his command whose sole purpose is the downfall of humanity. On the contrary, Papa Legba—as is the case with all the loas—helps people with matters of daily living, clears away obstacles in our path, and provides opportunities for improving our lives. That's a far cry from the cocaine-crazed baby snatcher portrayed in *American Horror Story: Coven.*

14

Père Antoine, the Inquisition and His Legendary Date Palm

Father Père Antoine approved of what Marie Laveau was doing because she would encourage Voodoos to come back to mass, unlike the other Voodoo leaders who discouraged their followers from going to Church.

—CHARLES GANDOLFO

It is highly unusual for a prominent Catholic priest to be associated with a renowned Voudou priestess. Yet here we are. We probably wouldn't be talking about Père Antoine were it not for his relationship with Marie Laveau. At least not in this book. It's his relationship with her that prompted me to look more into his life. It's not every day you can speak freely with your parish priest—who incidentally happened to be the official enforcer of the Spanish Inquisition in New Orleans—about the service to Damballah you will be conducting on a given day.

But Marie Laveau could speak openly to Father Antoine. She didn't hide her activities, and he didn't judge her and force her underground. In fact, they worked out an arrangement where she could use the yard behind St. Louis Cathedral for her Voudou ceremonies every Sunday so long as she came to church. And go to church she did, bringing the Voudous with her. In this way, she helped build an inclusive congregation that genuinely represented the community and not just the white Christian part.

Père Antoine served St. Louis Cathedral for over forty years as a Capuchin priest, from 1785 to 1790 and again from 1795 until he died in 1829. He was known for his charity work with Marie Laveau in ministering to the sick during the plagues of the 1800s, praying with the incarcerated, and providing spiritual comfort to men on death row. In addition to his work with the sick, Père Antoine shared Marie Laveau's dedication to helping the poor and enslaved.

As a general rule, Father Antoine was much beloved. However, he had his detractors and was controversial. He was rigid in his beliefs, considered a troublemaker, and known as the "scourge of religion in Louisiana" (Onofrio 1999). This criticism is not without merit, though it's hard to say which part of his story would comprise a "scourge." If it had anything to do with his fraternization with the Voudous and runaway slaves, I haven't found mention of it anywhere. Maybe it was the Great Fire that occurred in 1788, when he made the fateful decision not to ring the church bells as a warning.

It was Good Friday, and the Church forbade the ringing of church bells on that day. Despite knowing the fire was coming, he refused to ring the bell and warn the city. Before anyone knew what was happening, the entire city and the cathedral were engulfed in flames. A cornerstone for a new church was laid immediately after the fire, and in 1794, the new church was completed and designated a cathedral. Despite this disaster, Père Antoine was appointed to be its rector by the Spanish crown.

In addition to that display of rigid adherence to Church rules no matter the consequences, Père Antoine had a dark side. He was sent to New Orleans for the express purpose of being the Inquisition enforcer. Under the title "Vicar and Ecclesiastical Judge of New Orleans," the Tribunal of the Holy Office of the Inquisition in Cartagena, Spain, officially named him its commissary in Louisiana in 1786 (Pederson 2011). The Spanish Inquisition was initially intended to identify heretics among those converted from Judaism and Islam to Catholicism. For centuries, the Inquisition persecuted people who did not adhere to Orthodox Catholicism, specifically those they deemed heretics. Curiously, Antoine wound up being besties with Marie Laveau and assisting the Voudous and runaway slaves, while his Inquisition activities were on the extreme downlow or at least, for all intents and purposes, seemingly ineffective.

One of the challenges the Spanish authorities faced was selling Catholicism to New Orleanians. The Inquisition had been instrumental in Spain as a means of coercing and forcing conversion compliance. Even with the Louisiana Black Codes in place, the Church had to pursue its persecutory goals in secret in the mostly French city. Father Antoine's presence posed a threat politically. The local government knew that, should it become common knowledge that the Inquisition had arrived in New Orleans, immigration would be negatively impacted. They needed more citizens to build up New Orleans.

While Spain owned Louisiana, more than half its residents were French, so they knew they couldn't strong-arm their campaign in the open. Instead, their workaround involved officers waiting for someone pre-targeted as a heretic to travel outside the Louisiana colony to arrest them. Then, they would try the person elsewhere, and no one in New Orleans would be the wiser.

The powers that be had diverging opinions on religious freedom, as well as their opinions of Père Antoine. Immigrants to Louisiana were promised freedom of religious thought by Don Diego de Gardoqui, a Spanish politician and diplomat. Esteban Rodríguez Miró, governor of Louisiana at the time, would not agree to complete religious freedom. As an agreement was made that prompted a large emigration from western settlements, Antoine was not aware of the master plan behind the scenes to ship him back to Spain. He was considered problematic.

Antoine's leadership had been questioned by the auxiliary bishop Cyril de Barcelona, who had been investigating Antoine's activities for some time and had tried getting Antoine to vacate his position. True to form,

Father Antoine absolutely refused to leave his church, which resulted in "the schism of 1805." The bishop ultimately made a request to Governor Miro to deport Antoine back to Spain, and Miro seized on the opportunity to get rid of the problematic priest.

Père Antoine had a large following of Catholics who adored him in the city, so sending him away was not easy. It had to be a clandestine operation to remove him. Antoine had sent Miro a letter telling him of his appointment as agent of the Inquisition and that he might need a few officers to help him with his operations in the night. Shortly thereafter, he was awakened by an alarm. Seeing an officer and some grenadiers, Antoine naturally thought they had come in the night to assist him. He addressed the men, "My friends, I thank you and his excellency for the readiness of this compliance with my request. But I have no use for your services, and you shall be warned in time when you are wanted. Retire, then, with the blessing of God."

Much to his surprise, the soldiers instead arrested the friar, who exclaimed, "What! Will you dare lay your hands on a Commissary of the Holy Inquisition?"

An officer replied, "I dare obey orders," and promptly deposed Père Antoine from his home and onto a vessel bound the following day for Cadiz (Langford 1901).

One might wonder about the nature of the beef between the priest and the governor. Apparently, about a year before Antoine asked Miro for assistance with his covert Inquisition activities, the Spanish Tribunal had instructed Antoine to search and seize all subversive materials in the colony. Miro had become aware of Antoine's planned activities, which he believed would get in the way of growing the population in New Orleans, which was Miro's mission for the colony. Either that or Miro was guilty of having subversive materials himself and didn't want to get caught. Nevertheless, it provided the *force de jour* needed to remove Father Antoine, beloved priest be damned.

Father Antoine's congregation did not know their priest had been sent away without so much as a notice or a goodbye. Most of his congregation absolutely loved him because he was a champion for the underdog. He hung out with the poor and enslaved and in undesirable places like prisons and sick rooms. The people counted on him to help them and to show up whenever and wherever he was needed. So, when he didn't show up for Mass that day in 1805, his flock thought he may be sick and hurried to his little cabin behind the church to check on him. They learned of his dispute with the powers that be that resulted in his removal.

While Miro and the bishop were successful in deporting Antoine, their victory was short-lived. The people were angry and voted Père Antoine as their priest despite what the governor, bishop, or general said. A few years later, Antoine was sent back to New Orleans, where he continued to work as a secret agent of the Inquisition and priest to his congregation.

Antoine remained in service to his parish until his death on January 22, 1829, at the age of eighty-one. He was laid to rest in St. Louis Cathedral after one of the largest funeral services ever seen in the city. His death caused the entire city to go into mourning, whereupon even businesses closed. For three days, his body laid in wake in the cathedral rectory where thousands paid their respects. On the day of his funeral,

> The firing of a cannon announced the beginning of the ceremonies. The coffin was carried on the shoulders of four young men who were surrounded by eight honorary pallbearers, all friends of the deceased. (St. Louis Cathedral, n.d.)

Following his burial, the city council passed an ordinance pledging to wear black crepe on their arms in his honor for thirty days (Scott 2017). So great was his selfless concern for the wellbeing of others that his parishioners assumed he would achieve sainthood soon after his death. This belief was acted upon, as his home behind the church was dismantled piece by piece by folks wanting a holy relic. Barely anything remained within just a few days following his death.

Just like Marie Laveau, there are signs of Père Antoine's legacy in the city. The garden behind St. Louis Cathedral was dedicated to him and named after his namesake saint, St. Anthony. The alley on the northeast side of the cathedral, originally called St. Anthony's Alley, was renamed Père Antoine Alley in 1924.

As is typical of New Orleans's esteemed residents, Père Antoine's ghost is said to have remained in the city after the burial of his body. Sightings began almost immediately after his internment, with people describing apparitions of him with a shaven head, dressed as a monk in a long brown robe, and reading from his prayer book. To this day, his peaceful spirit can be observed wandering up and down the alleyway alongside the cathedral. He can be seen most frequently during quiet mornings whenever a dense fog flows in from the Mississippi River and blankets the French Quarter.

Should you be ever so fortunate as to witness the spirit of Père Antoine, consider yourself blessed in a big way. People who encounter him report a sense of well-being, calm, and compassion filling them. It is said to be a good omen to catch sight of Père Antoine in his alleyway. A sighting of his spirit is said to foretell glad tidings that are soon to come into the life of those to whom he appears.

PÈRE ANTOINE'S DATE PALM

Aside from weird Catholic politics, perhaps the most curious and sustaining story of Père Antoine involves the legend of the date palm tree that grew adjacent to his home. It was believed to have miraculous healing properties given its association with Father Antoine, particularly because of how he reportedly nurtured it during his lifetime. The tree, in fact, held such personal significance to him that he made provisions for its care in the event of his death. He wanted to be sure that the tree was never destroyed.

Père Antoine's date palm

The slightly creepy story begins with a bromance between Père Antoine and a man named Emile Jardin. The two men were such good friends that they were nearly inseparable: "One was never seen without the other; for they studied, walked, ate, and slept together" (Aldrich 1873, par. 3). One day, as they were preparing to enter the church, they were informed of the passing of a foreign woman who had recently moved into the neighborhood. She had been ill, and they had tended to her and were fond of her. Her death was nonetheless sudden and caught them by surprise.

The woman left a young girl named Anglice, of sixteen or seventeen years, without friends or family to take care of her. The two men felt sorry for the girl's predicament and decided to care for her as if she were their sister.

Now, Anglice was a striking, blonde-haired beauty that others seemed to pale next to in comparison. Over time, both Antoine and Emile secretly fell in love with the girl, though neither admitted to it. It became apparent that each of the men was increasingly distraught over their infatuations, which threatened their "ascetic dreams of heaven." There was no sign that she shared the sentiments of either man, however.

One night, Emile and Anglice went missing. This was of great concern to Antoine, not only because they were missing but also because he had failed to tell Anglice about his feelings for her. Apparently, his best friend beat him to the punch. As Antoine lifted his prayer book, a piece of paper fell out of the pages that read, "Ne soyez pas en colère. Par-donnez-nous, car nous aimons. (Don't be angry. Forgive us, for we love.)" (Aldrich 1873, par. 10).

Fast forward to about four years later when Antoine received a letter from Anglice that had been delayed due to a storm and shipwreck. In it, Anglice informed Antoine of Emile's passing. She begged him for forgiveness for leaving in the manner they did. She told him she was dying and that she and Emile had a child, also named Anglice. She asked him to look after the child for her upon her passing. Shortly thereafter—before he even had time to fully grieve for his friend—Anglice had died, and the daughter arrived at his doorstep. As he laid eyes upon her, his heart filled with joy. She looked so much like his beloved Anglice!

At first, the young girl had a hard time adjusting to her new home. She lost weight and became withdrawn. Doctors couldn't find anything physically wrong with her, and everyone assumed she missed her parents. Then, she seemed to come around and told Antoine that she indeed missed the island she called home. Two weeks later, she passed away. Heartbroken, Antoine buried her in his garden and spent all of his free time sitting next to her grave.

One day, he noticed a green sprout coming out of the grave. He didn't know what was growing there, but he let it grow until it became a tall willowy tree that resembled Anglice. A stranger passed and told Antoine that it was a beautiful date palm. When he learned it was a palm tree, he believed it had been sent to him by God: "Bon Dieu, vous m'avez donné cela (God, you gave me this)!" (Aldrich 1873)

From that time forward, he revered that palm tree, nurturing it daily as if it were Emile, Anglice, and child all rolled into one entity.

St. Anthony (photo courtesy of the author)

15

St. Anthony of Padua,
Patron Saint of Lost Things

*Earthly riches are like the reed. Its roots are sunk in the swamp, and
its exterior is fair to behold; but inside it is hollow. If a man leans
on such a reed, it will snap off and pierce his soul.*

—ST. ANTHONY OF PADUA

St. Anthony is the patron saint of lost things and guards against ship-
wrecks and starvation. He champions the poor and oppressed, barren
women, American Indians, elderly people, fishermen, harvests, horses, mail
delivery, sailors, and more. In some countries, St. Anthony is prayed to
by travelers and vacationers for a safe journey. According to some stories,
sailors keep a statue of St. Anthony on the mast of the ship and appeal
to him for safety while at sea. Whether in their official capacity with the
Church or in their folk capacity, all saints function as heavenly advocates
and protectors of nations, cities, places, occupations, people, and families.

The saints are found in several magico-spiritual contexts in New
Orleans, in addition to their official status in the Catholic Church. St.
Anthony is one of the most popular saints in New Orleans with such dual
Church and folk status. He is a saint of devotion in Catholicism, as well as
a folk saint in Voudou, hoodoo, and Catholic Conjure. Catholic Conjure
combines the mystical rites of the Catholic Church with the sacramentals

of folk Catholicism and the conjure workings of hoodoo. Some practitioners will also incorporate rites of the European grimoires in their practice.

For example, it is said that Voudou Queen Marie Laveau always kept a statue of St. Anthony in her front yard. When she was busy with spiritual work, she would turn the statue upside down. Her clients recognized the sign and knew not to disturb her as long as he remained in this position. As soon as she turned him upright, visitors again came a-callin' for her spiritual prescriptions and gris gris charms.

St. Anthony was a powerful Franciscan preacher and teacher who lived from 1195 until 1231 CE. He was born and raised by a wealthy family in Lisbon, Portugal, and died in Padua, Italy. His iconography typically depicts him as holding a lily and a book, often with the baby Jesus in his arms. His feast day is June 13, which is the anniversary of his death. Because he was buried on a Tuesday and many miracles occurred at that time, Tuesday is his celebrated day of the week. It is accepted practice to pray a Novena to him on thirteen consecutive Tuesdays.

Shortly after his death, people began praying to St. Anthony to find or recover lost and stolen articles. Nearly everywhere, he is asked to intercede with God for the return of things lost or stolen. Those familiar with him refer to him affectionately as "Tony" and may pray, "Tony, Tony, turn around. Something's lost and must be found." I have prayed this little ditty many times in my life, and he always answers, sometimes with impressive speed.

St. Anthony is traditionally invoked to find lost things because of an incident that happened in his own life. According to legend, he had a psalter that contained valuable information that he used in teaching students in his Franciscan Order. A novice who had grown tired of the religious life went AWOL and took St. Anthony's psalter with him. When St. Anthony realized his psalter was missing, he prayed for its safe return. Soon after his prayer, the thief felt compelled to return it to St. Anthony and return to the Order, which accepted him back.

Another, more colorful, version of St. Anthony's missing psalter suggests that the novice was stopped in his tracks by a ghastly devil wielding an ax who threatened to crush him if he did not return the book immediately (Alvarado 2017).

St. Anthony is well known among hoodoos. Practitioners commonly request his intercession to reconcile with a lost lover. He is typically petitioned with a brown candle, as brown is the color of his robe. An informant identified as the "Gifted Medium from New Orleans" in Harry Middleton Hyatt's seminal work, *Hoodoo-Conjuration-Witchcraft-Rootwork*, reported the following regarding burning candles to St. Anthony:

> They burn to St. Anthony for to bring people back, mens back to women, back when they done quit. You make a wish and burn that light to him. Go to the church anywhere and light a light if you don't have the saint at the house. If you have had the saint blessed and put at your home and you prays to it three times a day, that's to bring anybody back to you who done left you . . . say six in morning, twelve in the day, and six in the evening. That's three times, you pray to this saint. And have your light burning. In nine days, you see an improvement. (Hyatt 1970, 949)

Because St. Anthony finds lost people, his aid is also requested for lost souls. Believers call his name while visualizing their lost loved one. Then, they explain to the saint the importance of finding the missing person as they implore his aid. It is believed the missing person will be found after reciting the following prayer.

Prayer to Find What Is Lost

St. Anthony, when you prayed, your stolen book of prayers was given back to you. Pray now for all of us who have lost things precious and dear. Pray for all who have lost faith, hope, or the friendship of God. Pray for us who have lost friends or relatives by death. Pray for all who have lost peace of mind or spirit. Pray that we may be given new hope, new faith, new love. Pray that lost things, needful and helpful to us, may be returned to our keeping. Or, if we must continue in our loss, pray that we may be given Christ's comfort and peace. Amen.

St. Anthony was well known for his numerous miracles. His most famous miracle could well be his sermon to the fishes. As the story goes, one day, St. Anthony went to Rimini in Italy, known for its population of heretics. When he started preaching, they mocked him instead of listening to him. So, St. Anthony turned his back on them and stated, "Because you show yourself unworthy of God's word, behold, I turn to the fishes so that your unbelief may be shown up more clearly."

Standing on the shore, Anthony began preaching to the fish in the lake. As he shared how much God loved the creatures of the waters, a shoal of fish swam near, lifting their heads up from the water so they could hear him better. When St. Anthony was finished with his sermon, he blessed the fish, and they swam away. This event no doubt caught people's attention. Some witnesses responded by running to their friends and begging them to come and see for themselves what was happening, while others fell to their knees and wept.

Soon, St. Anthony was surrounded by people asking for his forgiveness. He then encouraged the people to renounce their sinful ways and embrace the teachings of God. Apparently, they did, and so it was that the city of Rimini was purged of heresy.

In the context of hoodoo, Voudou, and Catholic Conjure, it is customary to provide St. Anthony with offerings to sweeten him to the petitioner's cause. This is different from traditional Catholicism, which does not require any offerings to be made to a saint when petitioning them. Nevertheless, flowers, small votives, and written notes are commonly provided.

Hoodoo old-timers viewed St. Anthony as a player. For example, an informant from Algiers, Louisiana, stated in Hyatt's *Hoodoo-Conjuration-Witchcraft-Rootwork* that St. Anthony "laks cigahs and he was a good time man" (1970, 1221). A "good time man" back in the day would refer to your classic womanizer or gambler who likes to drink and party. Indeed, these are not behaviors characteristic of St. Anthony's life history—that we know of anyway.

Christian literature has been rewritten, chopped up, and filtered through an obvious agenda over time. In fact, many of the saints engaged in normal human behaviors at all ends of the spectrum. So, if St. Anthony were a "good time man" at some point in his life, it seriously would not be a shocker.

In New Orleans, Tallant (1946), Pitkin (1904), and Ellis (1965) all report that St. Anthony of Padua is petitioned as Yon Sue or Monsieur Agassou and that he manifests as a great guardian who protects Voudouists from those who would interfere with their freedom to worship the spirits of Africa. Agassou is petitioned for protection and for money. His vévé (ritual symbol), a statue of St. Anthony of Padua, and a figure of a spotted panther or leopard are used when petitioning him.

ST. ANTHONY'S GUIDE (S.A.G.) FOR SAFE DELIVERY

St. Anthony's Guide (S.A.G.) for Safe Delivery is one of my favorite folk sacramentals. I do this working with every package I ship and every letter I send. With the future of the United States Post Office currently in the balance as of summer 2020, this working warrants a quick revival, as it is a most useful sacramental to perform. To invoke the powers of St. Anthony for the safe delivery of your mail, write the letters "S. A. G." somewhere on your package or envelope prior to mailing. That's all there is to it.

Now, the origin of this story is pretty impressive. Long ago, in Spain in 1729, a merchant named Antonio Dante had his sights on starting a new business in Lima, Peru. So, he left Spain for South America. His wife, who had remained behind in Spain, wrote him numerous times, but she never received a reply. Needless to say, she became extremely concerned.

So, she wrote him a letter, went to church, and carefully tucked it into the sleeve of St. Anthony's statue while praying, "St. Anthony, I pray to thee; let this letter reach him and obtain for me a speedy reply." She had faith that St. Anthony would miraculously deliver her letter to her husband.

The next day, the merchant's wife returned to the church to check the statue and was distressed to see her letter still there. She shared her story with the sexton of the church, and he told her that had he tried to retrieve the letter, but it wouldn't come off the statue. When he asked her if she would try, she did and was able to easily remove the letter. Not only that, 300 gold coins fell to the ground! Upon closer inspection, she realized that it was not her own letter she held in her hands but one from her husband!

Several of the friars gathered around to witness the event and waited for the woman to open the letter, dated July 23, 1729. It read:

My dearest wife. For some time, I have been expecting a letter from you, and I have been greatly troubled and concerned at not hearing from you. But at last, your letter has come and given me joy. It was a Father of the Order of St. Francis who brought it to me. You complain that I have left your letters unanswered. I assure you that when I did not receive any from you, I believed you must be dead, and so you may imagine my happiness at the arrival of your letter. I answer you now by the same religious Father and send you three hundred golden crowns [coins], which should suffice for your support until my approaching return. In the hope of soon being with you, I pray God for you, and I commend myself to my dear patron St. Anthony, and ardently desire that you may continue to send me tidings of yourself. Your most affectionate, Antonio Dante. (Miracles of the Saints 2010)

To this day, the merchant's letter is preserved in the Franciscan Monastery at Oviedo. In memory of this miracle, people began marking their packages with S.A.G. to place them under the protection of St. Anthony and to ensure they make it safely to their destinations.

St. Anthony's patronage is astounding when you think about it. He nearly covers the gamut of human conditions. In addition to being a popular, canonized Catholic saint, he plays a significant role in New Orleans Voudou, and has done so for more than a hundred years. St. Anthony is petitioned as Yon Sue or Monsieur Agassou as a great guardian protector of religious freedom and cultural heritage, or he is petitioned for money and prosperity.

He serves as a cloak for St. Maroon in fights for justice. He stands in for Papa Legba when roads need opening and decisions need to be made. He plays an essential role in hoodoo, where he is petitioned for anything from finding lost people to reuniting lovers. Even when simply lighting a candle to him in the context of Catholicism or folk magick, you can be sure petitioners make a common request: St. Anthony, pray for us!

Altar to St. Expedite (photo courtesy of the author)

16

St. Expedite, Patron Saint of Instant Gratification

Procrastination is the bad habit of putting off until the day after tomorrow what should have been done the day before yesterday.

—Napoleon Hill

If he were alive today, we might find St. Expedite wearing spectacles while on a virtual battlefield of Russian hackers. Or perhaps we could find him fighting the good fight as a public defender, taking a knee for white-on-black crime, or working in a shelter for runaway youth. Indeed, St. Expedite is a saint of the people whose patronage has expanded with time. His function has adapted to the ever-changing social climate, making him incredibly relevant among computer programmers, sorcerers, and social justice warriors alike. Anyone who petitions him with a sincere heart and the promise of a piece of pound cake—Sara Lee, preferably—will receive his intercession.

St. Expedite is on the fringe of Catholicism through no fault of his own. Nonetheless, he is much loved in New Orleans Voudou and in folk Catholicism. Originally, he was Expeditus, a Roman centurion in Armenia who was martyred on April 19, 303, for converting to Christianity. When he decided to convert from paganism, legend tells of the devil disguised as a raven who tried to convince him to put off his conversion until the next day. But Expeditus resisted, exclaiming, "I'll be a Christian today!" as he stomped on the raven and killed it.

This story is where his patronage against procrastination originates. Unfortunately, Expeditus was beheaded during the Diocletian Persecution in Melitene (modern-day Malatya, Turkey), meeting the same fate as many Christian converts preceding him. Consequently, he became known as Sant-Espedito di Melitene or Saint Expedite of Melitene. His association with death made him the ideal saint to syncretize with the Voudou spirits of death, Baron Samedi in New Orleans Voudou and Baron LaCroix in Haitian Vodou.

Whenever there is a discussion about St. Expedite, the topic invariably winds up with the question of his origin story. His story in New Orleans begins with the construction of the Our Lady of Guadalupe Chapel, International Shrine of St. Jude (Old Mortuary Chapel). Built in 1826 as a funeral chapel for victims of yellow fever, Our Lady of Guadalupe Chapel was strategically constructed near St. Louis Cemetery No. 1 to minimize the spread of disease throughout the French Quarter. The unknown dead were moved through the mortuary's back door directly into the cemetery right across the street.

According to one legend, in the early 1900s, some priests sent off to Spain for a large statue of the Virgin Mary, and, months later, two crates arrived by ship. One crate contained the statue of Mary, which was expected. The other crate, however, had the word "ESPEDITO" stamped on the outside. When the priests opened the second crate, they found the statue of a saint depicted as a Roman centurion. Apparently, the priests did not recognize the saint's identity and mistook the stamp for the name of the saint. And so, the unidentified statue of the Roman centurion has been known as St. Expedite ever since—or so the story goes.

Another version of his origin story is told by Father Dan Cambria of the Divine Mercy Chapel in New Orleans. He says Ursuline nuns received an unidentified statue from France just prior to the French Revolution in—you guessed it—a wooden crate. On the outside of the crate was the word "EXPEDITE." The nuns opened the box and did not recognize the saint, so they asked the bishop, and he didn't know either. So, they wrote a letter to the folks who had sent the crate, asking about the statue's identity. Unfortunately, they never received an answer, as the French Revolution had begun. As a result, the nuns called him St. Expedite and placed the statue at the end of a corridor of their school where it remained for several decades.

Because his location was actually in a small, out-of-the-way niche, he could have easily been forgotten by the nuns. But St. Expedite is a likeable guy. He was neither forgotten nor ignored. The students and the nuns living in the convent took a liking to him. They prayed to him and eventually developed what is referred to as the Nine-Hour Flying Novena to St. Expedite. It seemed they only got positive results when praying to him in this manner, so needless to say his devotion continued to grow and, with it, his legendary reputation for bringing unusually quick results.

 Scan the QR code with your Android or iPhone to find detailed instructions for performing the Nine-Hour Novena to St. Expedite or visit *www.crossroads-university.com.*

Father Dan suggested that this legend was a "light-hearted" story and that the feast day for St. Expedite might be April Fool's Day, instead of the date of his martyrdom, April 19. Clearly, Father Dan does not recognize St. Expedite as an official saint in Catholicism; but at least he concedes that when people pray to St. Expedite, they get results, and quick ones at that (Alvarado 2014).

Curiously, St. Expedite's origin story is recounted with a similar theme across the globe. In my book, *The Conjurer's Guide to St. Expedite,* I recount one such story about his arrival in France:

Once upon a time, in approximately 1781, Paris, France, a crate containing the body of a saint from the Denfert-Rochereau catacombs in Paris was delivered to a community of nuns there. The catacombs, known as "The World's Largest Grave," are underground ossuaries that hold the remains of approximately 6 million people. The catacombs were created at the end of the 18th century and are contained in a renovated section of caverns and tunnels that are the remains of Paris' historical stone mines (Musée de France, n.d.). The crate received by the nuns had the word SPEDITO written on it. In this story, the nuns make un petit faux pas, attributing SPEDITO for the name of the martyr. When they prayed to St. Expedite for his intercession, their prayers were answered so quickly that reports of his rapid response spread like wildfire throughout Catholic countries. Thus began the concerted effort to spread a cult of devotion to "the saint who could make things happen in a hurry." (Alvarado 2013, 18)

St. Expedite has a similar origin story on the tiny French Island of Réunion, located off the east coast of Madagascar in the Indian Ocean. Apparently, a mysterious crate was received by some nuns there. In their origin story, the crate was full of bones, not a statue. Because the box of old bones arrived with ESPEDITO stamped on the wooden box, those who received them assumed they were the bones of a saint and named him St. Expedite.

St. Expedite is also found in the largely Sicilian and Italian community of Independence, Louisiana. There, he is referred to as St. Expedito. He became popular in the community when a chapel was built in the late 1940s in his honor after he helped someone in a big way. According to Karen Williams:

In the '50s and '60s the pavilion was packed with people eating and drinking. Differing from New Orleans' custom of feeding the saint, the Italians made sure to feast with him, not limiting the food to one simple cake to leave for the saint's benefit, but feasting on hotdogs garnished with a local specialty, Hi Ho barbeque sauce, made in the community, along with soft drinks and beer, while the festivities included dancing and music by local bands like the Rhythm Kings. (Williams 2011, par. 8, lines 8–14)

The chapel in Independence is aptly called St. Expedito and is complete with a couple of portraits of the saint, plaster appendages representing body parts that had been healed (reminiscent of St. Roche in New Orleans), and, of course, a statue. There was actually a St. Expedito Society active there for eighty years. During the 1980s, celebrations used to be held every second Sunday in June in honor of the saint; although, as membership in the society waned, so did the activities (Marciano 2005, as cited in Williams 2011). The chapel apparently remains and is used periodically for special functions.

Despite similar origin stories from around the world, St. Expedite is unfortunately embroiled in controversy. Of course, his origins are questioned by the Catholic Church, but it wasn't always that way. He was included twice in the 5th-century *Martyrologium Hieronymianum* (*Martyrology of Jerome*), which consists of names of individuals considered saints and martyrs, arranged according to the calendar order of feast days and anniversaries. The first entry for St. Expedite was made on April 18, and the second on April 19. It is believed the first entry was a mistake, given he was beheaded on April 19, since it is customary to designate a saint's date of death as the official feast day.

Even though such mistakes were commonplace in the martyrologies, some folks questioned his existence and concluded that both entries were simply typos. Thus, some consider him an imaginary saint. This bizarre assertion, coupled with the fact that no official relics exist for St. Expedite, fueled Church skepticism in the early 20th century. The Second Vatican Council (1962–1965) decided to remove St. Expedite from the universal liturgical calendar, and, just like that, the wonder saint was reduced to a crate and a mistake (Alvarado 2013).

The legend of St. Expedite is reflected in his iconography. For example, he is called Expedite from the Latin Expeditus, which refers to a category of Roman foot-soldiers who march with a light load (O'Brien 2004) and can therefore move quickly. In one hand, he holds a palm frond, which is the Christian symbol for martyrdom. His other holds a cross inscribed with the word "hodie"—which is Latin for "today"—stretched above his head. A crow or raven clutching a ribbon in its beak, upon which is written the word "cras," meaning "tomorrow" in Latin, is stomped beneath the saint's foot.

In the folklore of many cultures, crows and ravens are considered to be portents of death. The association with crows and ravens, coupled with St. Expedite's placement in a mortuary chapel, solidifies his association with death and dying. Two-headed conjure doctors and sorcerers strongly identify with these aspects of his character. St. Expedite's imagery is slightly different in Germany. He is shown pointing at a clock, portraying the same message of avoiding procrastination.

Despite being treated as a novelty by the Catholic Church, St. Expedite is one of the most popular and beloved saints in New Orleans and, indeed, the world over. No amount of slander and storytelling can make him fade into obscurity. And seriously, what's not to love? His name places him squarely on the divine side of instant gratification as he is petitioned for prompt solutions to business problems, winning court cases, securing employment, making wishes, and finding a lover. He is even embraced by the world of Internet technology as patron saint to computer programmers and hackers. Moreover, St. Expedite has become increasingly popular among conjure doctors in the growing practice of Catholic Conjure. In fact, he has been a fixture in the tradition of folk Catholicism in Louisiana for many years.

Needless to say, St. Expedite is more alive and well than ever in today's world. His veneration takes on many forms, including small shrines and diminutive temples of devotion called *edicolae* along rural paths and roadsides, as well as home altars and sacred spaces devoted entirely to him. So long as he continues to be the saint that will grant any request in record time for a mere slice of pound cake and a couple of red roses, St. Expedite will remain the common man's saintly bro—a saint of the people.

St. Joseph at the Altar of the Holy Kinship, c. 1520, Salzburg, Austria. (This file is licensed under the Creative Commons Attribution-Share Alike 4.0 International license.)

17

St. Joseph, Family Man

We are born to love, we live to love, and we will die to love still more.

—St. Joseph

St. Joseph is everybody's daddy. He is known as San Jose in Latinx communities and San Giuseppe in Italian neighborhoods. He has also earned the nickname St. Joe in New Orleans. He is highly venerated in New Orleans, and on St. Joseph's Day (March 19), he is honored with lavish altars, good food, and celebration. He stands beside Black Hawk, Moses, and Dr. Martin Luther King in the spiritual churches as a patron saint of social justice, and he is a favorite saint in Italian folk magick. St. Joseph is associated with the Voudou loa, Ogun Balindio, a healer.

The main sources of information we have about St. Joseph's life are the first chapters of the first and third Gospels. He is considered the patron saint of families, fathers, pregnant women, travelers, immigrants, house buyers and sellers, craftsmen, engineers, and the working class. Within the Roman Catholic tradition, St. Joseph is honored as the husband of Mary and earthly father of Jesus Christ. In this position, he was head of the household.

He is considered the patron saint of families in New Orleans and enjoys influence over several areas of life, including finding a job and selling or renting a house and real estate. He is petitioned by fathers, as well as single mothers, who are both mother and father to their children.

St. Joseph is a sympathetic defender of lovelorn men—so guys, if you get your heart broken, St. Joe is the one who can help you feel better. He can also help to bring your partner back to the path of fidelity when they have lost their way. New Orleanians who suspect their wives of adultery will often come to St. Joseph for his help. They reason that since *his* wife had someone else's baby, he will understand their plight and come to their aid.

Joseph is also the unofficial patron against doubt and hesitation; perhaps this was the Church's attempt to replace St. Expedite. Since St. Expedite was ousted from the list of official Catholic saints, there was a need to fill the gap in patronage as a result.

Legend says that Joseph died in the arms of Jesus and Mary, receiving grace at the moment of death. Thus, he is the patron saint of a happy death, as well.

In New Orleans, there are parades akin to the marching clubs and truck parades of Mardi Gras and St. Patrick's Day in honor of St. Joseph. Some groups of Mardi Gras Indians stage their last procession of the season on the Sunday prior to St. Joseph's Day, otherwise known as "Super Sunday," after which their costumes are taken apart.

ST. JOSEPH ALTARS

Between 1850 and 1870, New Orleans was a major port of entry for Sicilian immigrants. The U.S. Census Bureau estimates that there were more Italians concentrated in the city than in any other U.S. city. When the Sicilians came, they brought the tradition of St. Joseph altars with them.

The first St. Joseph altar was built in New Orleans in 1967 by members of the Greater New Orleans Italian Cultural Society (GNOICS). The tradition expanded to his feast day and continued yearly until it became the citywide event it is today. The origin of this practice can be traced back to the Middle Ages, when starvation was rampant, and Joseph was petitioned for relief. The altars were an act of gratitude for his intercession. The families of farmers and fishermen built simple altars in their homes to share their good fortune with others. Tradition dictates that no expense should be incurred to build the altar, and no profit should be made from it. This explains why on St. Joseph's feast day the altars are so elaborately built.

Italian Catholics and many descendants of Italian immigrants continued the tradition of St. Joseph tables, *tavole di San Giuseppe,* to honor the saint. The Feast of St. Joseph is a citywide celebration and includes public and private showings of altars built for the occasion. Notices are posted in newspapers and in other media inviting the public to view and partake of the traditional meal. Feast day altars are typically large, three-tiered, and elaborately decorated.

Because the Feast of St. Joseph occurs during Lent, there is no meat on the altars, only fish. The fish represent the twelve apostles, Jesus, and the miracles of the loaves of bread and fish. The fish also serves as a reminder of the Last Supper. In addition to fish, there are fruits, vegetables, salads, wine, cakes, cookies, stuffed artichokes, blessed breads, fava beans, and symbolic pastries. Usually, anyone who wishes to pay homage to St. Joseph at one of the participating homes at this time is allowed to do so.

St. Joseph tables are placed in both churches and homes. Each table is blessed by a priest and presided over by a statue of St. Joseph. A stalk of lily blossoms, votive candles, and a lace tablecloth are typically used to decorate the feast table. St. Joseph altars are especially famous for their blessed St. Joseph bread. The bread is sculpted into various shapes and is edible, while the symbolic pastries are not. It is said that during terrible storms, a piece of St. Joseph's blessed bread can be tossed outside, a prayer recited, and the storm will subside.

Aside from the St. Joseph's bread, the most important items on an altar are the lucky fava beans. A small piece of bread, a lucky bean, and sometimes a bay leaf or two are given to every visitor. Each of these items represents abundance, luck, prosperity, and protection.

At the conclusion of the event, the altars are dismantled, and the food is distributed to charity. Participants often leave donations at the table, with the proceeds going to cover the cost of the prepared food and the excess donated to charity.

BURYING A ST. JOSEPH STATUE TO SELL A HOME

By far the most well-known, wondrous work of St. Joseph is his ability to assist in the sale of real estate—especially homes. Over the years, there developed a tradition of St. Joseph having this special power in real estate transactions and home sales due to his association with family and carpentry. However, the formal tradition of burying St. Joseph in the earth began hundreds of years ago in Europe.

When an order of nuns needed more land for a convent, they buried medals of St. Joseph in the ground and prayed to him for help. They were apparently successful, and so, hoping for a little heavenly intercession, thousands of home sellers and real estate agents nationwide perform a ritual in which a statue of St. Joseph is buried upside down on a property to make it sell quickly.

To do this yourself, make a hole in the ground that is large enough to bury the St. Joseph statue vertically. Be sure to wrap him in plastic or place him in a plastic baggie because once your home sells, you will need to dig him up to keep him in your new home. Place the statue upside down in the ground. Face the upside-down statue *toward* the home that is to be sold. Pray the St. Joseph novena for nine consecutive days.

Once the home is sold, remove the statue from the ground. Display the statue in the heart of your new home. Oftentimes, folks will place him on the kitchen windowsill.

There are many such folk sacramentals associated with St. Joseph. It's no wonder, given his popularity. He takes care of business. He is the patron saint of families, a happy death, finding a job, and real estate. He is petitioned by fathers and single mothers and is a sympathetic defender of men whose hearts have been broken. He heals infidelity in marriages, reuniting couples who have lost their way. The Feast of St. Joseph remains a citywide celebration, and I don't foresee that changing anytime soon. St. Joseph may be the earthly father of Jesus, but the truth is, he's everybody's daddy.

St. Peter with keys on an altar for Marie Laveau (photo courtesy of the author)

18

St. Peter with Keys, Open da Do'

What matters is not your outward appearance . . . but your inner disposition.
Cultivate inner beauty, the gentle gracious kind that God delights in.

—St. Peter

St. Peter was an extremely popular saint back in the days of Marie Laveau. He served quite handily as the saint under which the Vodusi cloaked the spirit of Papa Legba. Both the saint and the spirit hold keys to locks, chains, and doors that function as obstacles to our success. While St. Peter began as the syncretized saint for Legba as a result of the Catholic imposition, he eventually earned a place for himself, independent of Papa Legba. The Catholic saint and the Voudou spirit have no problems coexisting in the inclusive spiritual tradition that is New Orleans Voudou.

St. Peter's true and original name was Simon, sometimes occurring in the form Symeon. The apostle Andrew was his brother, and the apostle Philip came from the same town, Bethsaida. Peter was personally installed as head of the apostles by Christ. He is considered the first pope.

St. Peter's iconography tells us who he is and what he represents in Catholicism. Among his sacred symbols are a shepherd's staff, which represents Peter's role as chief shepherd of Jesus's flock. When Jesus stood on the shore of the sea of Galilee after his resurrection, he instructed Peter to "Feed my lambs, tend my sheep" (John 21:15–17). In this way, Jesus formally left the responsibility of leading his flock and passing on his ministry to Peter.

A cock or rooster crowing represents Peter's threefold denial of Jesus in the courtyard of the high priest (Matthew 26:69–75). Keeping a rooster on the altar with St. Peter serves to remind him to not be a punk-ass bitch. Further, roosters are good for Papa Legba as well, so you are killing two birds with one stone here if you are a practitioner concerned with discovery.

Another symbol associated with St. Peter is the upside-down cross. The upside-down cross symbolizes the kind of cross upon which Peter was crucified during Emperor Nero's reign of Christian persecution (64–68 CE). Apparently, Peter stated to his executioners that he was not worthy of being crucified in the same manner as Jesus and that he should be killed in a different way, so upside down it was.

In hoodoo, interestingly enough, there is the practice of standing statues of saints on their heads when petitioning them, particularly if they have failed to come through on a petition. In that case, the statue of the saint is stood on its head until the prayers are answered. Some say this is supposed to be a form of punishment. After the prayer is answered, the saint is returned to an upright position and thanked in a public forum. Some folks find this particular practice uncomfortable, but it is more common than you might think. What's more, it seems to be effective.

St. Peter has quite a few more symbols that represent different aspects of his life story. For example, because Peter is the rock upon which the Church was built (Matthew 16:18), he is represented by a rock protruding from the sea. Because he was called by Jesus to be a fisher of men (Luke

5:10), he is associated with fishing nets. He is associated with boats because boats symbolize the Church with Peter at the helm (Matthew 8:23–27; 14:28–32). He is associated with the three-bar cross because it symbolizes the first office Peter held. And he is associated with chains because an angel set him free by loosening his chains when he was imprisoned (Acts 12:6–7).

Sometimes St. Peter's symbols are combined with a pair of keys that overlap and cross or are side by side. This is seen with the upside-down cross and the three-bar cross associated with St. Peter. Keys are among the chief attributes for which St. Peter is noted in New Orleans Voudou and hoodoo. He is referred to as St. Peter with Keys when he is petitioned for road-opening works, which are designed to open doors to opportunities and remove obstacles. He is also petitioned in this capacity to close certain doors, say to a bad relationship. Keys can both lock and unlock and are considered accordingly in folk magick traditions like hoodoo and conjure. Keys are routinely offered to images of St. Peter for his protection and blessings.

Much of St. Peter's story in the world of hoodoo is told by informants interviewed by Harry Middleton Hyatt in his seminal work, *Hoodoo-Conjuration-Witchcraft-Rootwork*. Just like St. Anthony and St. Joseph, St. Peter is petitioned using time-honored folk sacramentals. For example, there is the practice in New Orleans of carrying a talisman called the Saint Peter Protection Key. Essentially, it is a silver skeleton key that is anointed with Holy Oil. The key is simply placed in front of a statue of St. Peter or a religious icon of him that has been printed out and framed, and St. Peter is asked to bless the key. It is then carried for good luck and protection.

Another practice is to print out an image of St. Peter holding keys. Just do a Google search and find something you like. Get a nice gold frame and put the image in the frame. Then, make a little packet of nine guinea seeds out of red flannel, sew it closed, and attach it to the back

Find an image of St. Peter, such as this one, to hang on the back of your front door

of the frame. This practice is called "feeding the saint." Then hang the image of St. Peter on the back of your front door. This way, he will keep the doors open to opportunities and closed to miscreants and negative Nancies.

Now, some folks use a brass key when working with St. Peter as a saint of thieves. Say you suspect someone in your home of stealing some money from you. You can take a brass key and stick it into the Bible at the book of Revelation, then stand the Bible on end on a table or hold it up by the corners. Pray "By St. Peter, by St. Paul, by the Good Lord who made us all, if (name of suspect) has taken (name what was stolen), may (name of suspect) spin and fall." Repeat, calling out the name of each suspect; if you say the name of the guilty party, the Bible will fall over or the key will fall out. That brass key holds the secrets of thieves.

Crossed Keys of St. Peter (Hyatt 1970–1978, vol. 4, 3616)

In addition to the silver Protection Key and the brass Key of Secrets is the Crossed Keys of St. Peter. The pair of overlapping keys represent Peter's authority as the leader of the twelve apostles and the head of the early Church. Often, one key is silver while the other one is gold. The silver key represents his power to bind and loose temporal authority on earth. The gold key represents his power to bind and loose spiritual authority in heaven.

After Peter made his profession of faith in Jesus as the Messiah and the Son of the living God (Matthew 16:16), Jesus said, "I will give you the keys to the kingdom of heaven. Whatever you bind on earth shall be bound in heaven; and whatever you loose on earth shall be loosed in heaven" (Matthew 16:19). The keys also represent the authority to absolve sins or, in extreme cases when sins are not loosed, to excommunicate.

Two brass skeleton keys are crossed, as in the above illustration. They are held up in this position each morning. While standing in the morning sunrise, tell the keys which doors and mysteries you would have them unlock. When you are done, uncross the keys and lay them in front of an image of St. Peter. Be sure to keep the keys pointed upward, as this symbolically represents unlocking the gates of heaven.

Interestingly, there are people whom Hyatt interviewed who reported being scared to death of St. Peter. To them, he is a snitch and a pyromaniac, and if you have any sort of illegal dealings and you call upon St. Peter, he will have you locked up in a flash. And he just might burn your house down! They say to avoid him at all costs:

St. Peter, he don't mean nobody—don't mean no women no good. He's—he likes men—he likes policemen—he likes the judges, the jurymen. He'll keep you in trouble all the time. If you go to jail, he'll keep you in jail. He'll keep the door fastened against you if you pray to him and got him in your house—got him up over your door and you don't know no better. . . . He makes the landlord put you out—he go against you with the neighbors—he'll keep up confusion in your home—he'll set your house a fire. I had him in my house and I never had a fire in my house in my life until I got St. Peter. (Hyatt 1970–1978, vol. 2, 1406)

My guess is that the suspicious attitude toward St. Peter must be related to his denial of Jesus. This denial would cause a serious distrust of his character.

The main idea with St. Peter is that his key is like a double-edged sword. Yes, his key can unlock the door for you, but he can also close the door on you. And for no apparent reason, he seems to lock people up in jail and set their houses on fire! I don't know where these beliefs about St. Peter come from. They do not seem to have been present back when Marie Laveau was alive, as she is reported to have had a statue of St. Peter on her altar. He is also recorded as being summoned in her rituals and in Hoodoo Opening ceremonies.

I personally have not ever experienced anything negative with St. Peter. I do not doubt these old-timers experienced what they experienced and who knows why they energized St. Peter in such a manner. Perhaps it wasn't St. Peter at all but another spirit who was finding refuge behind the mask of St. Peter. From a practitioner's perspective, it is not uncommon for people who do not know what they are doing or who are ill advised to end up summoning a completely different spirit or energizing an aspect of a spirit that they are ill prepared to manage. One of the biggest mistakes people make when petitioning spirits with opening abilities is forgetting to ask the spirit or saint to close the door. This essentially leaves a portal to the spirit world open to whomever and whatever wants to come through and wreak havoc among the living.

Whether favored as a Catholic saint or hoodoo folk saint, St. Peter has held a prominent position in New Orleans for at least two hundred years. He functions effectively as a crossover saint—beloved as much by faithful Catholic churchgoers as by traditional conjure workers and Voudouists. Because he was the first leader of the early church, he is the most prominent apostle. And because he stands in place for Papa Legba when needed and is favored by Marie Laveau, he maintains a prominent place in New Orleans Voudou, as well.

Prosthetics, crutches, and other health apparatus left by visitors at St. Roche cemetery.
(Photo by Infrogmation, 2016. This file is licensed under the Creative Commons Attribution-Share Alike
4.0 International license.)

19

St. Roch, New Orleans's Own Patron Saint of Pandemics

Saint Roch, and all ye holy Confessors, pray for us.

—PRAYER TO ST. ROCH

One of the more unique saints with a beautiful and visually macabre presence in New Orleans is St. Roch (pronounced "rock"). His chapel at St. Roch Campo Santo Cemetery is believed by many to have healing qualities, which explains, in part, why people leave their prosthetics, crutches, and other health apparatus there after visiting. It is a small structure with seven pews; replicas of human organs hang on one wall, beneath which are the crutches, braces, and artificial limbs that people have left behind when healed of their afflictions. On yet another wall are hundreds of tiny plaques that say "thank you" to the saint.

In New Orleans, St. Roch is the special protector against plagues and epidemics and, by extension, pandemics. He is one of New Orleans's proven miracle workers. Over the years, thousands of people have been miraculously cured after making a pilgrimage to his chapel and asking for his intercession. He is the patron saint of dogs and dog lovers, surgeons, gravediggers, second-hand merchants, the falsely accused, tile makers, and diseased cattle. He is popular with unmarried women who pray to him for husbands.

There is also a hidden side to St. Roch that is unbeknownst to many. Some say that though he will give you what you want, he will also take something away—sometimes a beloved—so be careful what you ask for.

According to the *Golden Legend* or *Legenda Aureal*, a collection of hagiographies by Jacobus de Voragine written circa 1259–1266, Roch was born in Montpellier, France, to a wealthy, noble family. His birth is considered miraculous because his mother was barren until she prayed to the Virgin Mary. He was born with a birthmark on his chest in the form of a red cross, believed to be evidence of a miracle; especially given that the cross grew as he grew.

Like so many saints, we don't have much information about St. Roch's life. We know that when he was twenty years old, his parents died. His father, on his deathbed, ordained Roch governor of Montpellier. Roch used his status and fortune to care for the poor and the sick and gave away all his money. He passed on his governorship of Montpellier to his uncle and then set out for Italy in the guise of a beggar.

On the way, Roch stopped at Aquapendente, which had been stricken by the plague. He devoted himself to the afflicted, curing them with prayer, the touch of his hand, and the sign of the cross. Everywhere he went, the plague disappeared when confronted by his miraculous powers.

Despite his ability to heal others, however, Roch contracted the plague. He was shunned by a fearful community and kicked out of town. He then retreated to the forest, where he built a hut among lush greens watered by a spring that miraculously sprung from there. He became very ill, and during this time of quarantine, a hunting dog from a nearby manor befriended him. Each day, the dog would bring him bread to eat and lick the sores on his body until they healed.

After a lengthy recovery time, Roch finally returned home to Montpellier, but no one recognized him when he did. It is unclear as to whether he wore a disguise or people simply couldn't identify him, as both versions of the story exist. In any event, he was charged with false impersonation and spying, subsequently arrested on the orders of his uncle, and imprisoned for five years with his trusty canine companion. Together they ministered to others until the time of his death on August 16, 1327, while still in prison.

When he died, there appeared on the prison wall the name "Roch," written by an angelic hand in golden letters, along with the prediction that all who asked for his intercession would be delivered from the plague. When Roch's uncle heard about the divine event, he came to the prison to see for himself. Roch's grandmother also came to the prison to identify his body, which she did by noting the red cross on his chest. They gave him a glorious funeral and had a church built in his honor where his body was ultimately entombed.

Eighty-seven years after his death, a plague broke out in the city of Constance in 1414. The Fathers of the Council of Constance ordered public prayers and processions in honor of St. Roch, just as Father Thevis would do many years later. Immediately, the plague ceased!

In 1485, St. Roch's relics were secreted to Venice, where they are still venerated (Cleary 1912). Certain portions of his relics are also kept in Rome, Italy, and Arles, France. St. Roch is one of several saints with an entire cemetery devoted to him in New Orleans.

ST. ROCH CAMPO SANTO CEMETERY

During the 1800s, new immigrants arrived at New Orleans from Ireland, Italy, Spain, and Germany. Catholic Mass was in Latin, and there were no priests fluent in German at the time. So, the archdiocese sent for a German priest on behalf of the German Congregation of Holy Trinity. Father Peter Leonard Thevis arrived to meet the needs of the congregation.

Unfortunately, Father Thevis could not have arrived at a worse time. Cholera and yellow fever epidemics caused up to four hundred people to die each week, earning New Orleans the nickname "The Wet Grave." Things got so bad that Father Thevis invoked St. Roch's intercession. He promised the saint that he would build a chapel in his name if he would spare his parishioners. Legend holds that all of his parishioners avoided the scourge of yellow fever, so the chapel was built on land Father Thevis purchased from the heirs of Jack Phillips.

The chapel was dedicated on August 16, 1876, and it quickly became a pilgrimage site for people from all over the world suffering from health problems. Answered prayers resulted in people leaving replicas of healed body parts, braces, crutches, and prostheses as offerings of gratitude. The chapel is littered with such *ex votos*, lending to the gothic architecture a layer of haunting surrealism.

Located at 725 St. Roch Avenue, the cemetery is the resting place of Father Thevis, who died on August 21, 1893. He was buried under the floor in front of the altar. The inscription over the chapel door reflects the promise he made to St. Roch: "Erected by Vow 1875."

If you listen carefully, you can hear whispers of Voudou activity in St. Roch Cemetery. For years, the cemetery has held a prominent place in the sacred geography of the city as a popular ritual space for Voudou and hoodoo practitioners. Doctor Jean Montenée is buried there, after all. And Marie Laveau is known for conducting her hoodoo business in St. Roch Cemetery—for court cases and legal issues, in particular. Any worker worth their weight in red brick dust will have at least one cemetery, if not several cemeteries, where they do their magick rituals. Larger, older cemeteries are ideal, as they are often unmonitored, and the crumbling tombs and wall ovens make ideal makeshift altars from the Voudouists' points of view.

As a matter of record, St. Roch Cemetery's reputation as a Voudou cemetery goes back many years. Louie Haley, the sexton of the cemetery during the late 1930s, described it in an interview by the Federal Writers' Project (FWP):

> We've found plenty of stuff in this place, and mostly in the back, in the
> nigga section. I've found 'em burying tongues all stuck up with needles
> and pins and wrapped around wit' black thread. A lemon split and

sprinkled wit' black and red pepper and a note stuck in it. Once I found a pair of tan shoes wit' a note stuck between the heel and the sole, and on the note was written, "Willie, I want your death." Another time we found three hearts and still another time, a loaf of bread and poke chops sprinkled with black pepper and pins stuck in it. (Dillon, Folder 044)

In the 1800s, Voudou Queen Marie Laveau gathered grave dirt from St. Roch Cemetery for use in her conjures. She would gather a couple of handfuls and put it through a sifter to reduce it to a fine powder. The bigger pieces she would grind with her mortar and pestle until the dirt was smooth as silk. All the while, she would recite special psalms and prayers to empower the dirt with her intentions. This carefully prepared dirt was her graveyard dust.

Marie Laveau's St. Roch graveyard dust was a hot commodity for young girls seeking husbands. The Voudou Queen would sprinkle that powerful magickal dust over her female clients' heads so they would be lucky in love. Additionally, it was "brought by slaves to their young mistresses to be sprinkled with dexterity on the heads of those they wished for husbands." Indeed, one must be careful with whom one walks into St. Roch's cemetery because "once a man and a maid walk together there, they are sure to fall in love and be married" (*Times* 1938, 11).

A variety of folk Catholic traditions and legends are associated with the beautiful little chapel located on the cemetery grounds. Grease from the bell is considered powerful gris gris. The chapel is the site of Good Friday worship that is well known throughout the city. In celebration of the Passion of Christ, Catholics visit nine local churches, stopping to pray at each and ending at St. Roch's Cemetery at 3:00 p.m., the hour of our Lord's death. Some people put rocks in their shoes to increase the suffering of their pilgrimage.

On the chapel wall is the following prayer, written in both French and English:

O, great St. Roch, deliver us, we beseech thee, from the scourges of God.
Through thy intercessions, preserve our bodies from contagious diseases,
and our souls from the contagion of sin. Obtain for us salubrious air; but,
above all, purity of heart. Assist us to make good use of health, to bear
suffering with patience, and, after thy example, to live in the practice
of penance and charity that we may one day enjoy the happiness which
thou hast merited by thy virtues. St. Roch, pray for us (three times).

Because of St. Roch's reputation for coming through with petitions, it became customary for young women seeking good husbands to visit the shrine and burn a candle to him, imploring his intercession in the matter. On Good Friday, unmarried women visit nine churches, say a prayer, and make an offering at each one. They then visit St. Roch's Chapel and make the Stations of the Cross, which are situated in grotto-like wall niches built into the exterior walls.

The stations take the prayerful through Jesus's experiences with conviction, crucifixion, and burial. The women approach each station, where they genuflect and pray. Finally, they light a candle at the altar. It is believed that they would be happily married before the end of the year (*Los Angeles Times* 1926, 4).

THE VOUDOU HOODOO SAINT

St. Roch is recognized in the spiritual traditions of New Orleans, including Voudou and hoodoo. There are several rites associated with him in both traditions. New Orleans Voudou centers on the healing of the body, mind, and spirit, and so it is not a great leap to find St. Roch smack dab in the center of the tradition. He fits well with the New Orleans Voudou pantheon as the patron saint of infectious diseases, pandemics, and the sick and dying. He is syncretized with Babalú Aye, the Yoruban orisha of healing and protector of health. Just as in folk Catholicism, hoodoo drives unmarried women, in particular, to go to St. Roch to petition him for husbands. Since most end up married, the belief in him is strong (Dadswell 1946, 16).

As a hoodoo saint, St. Roch has the reputation of an eccentric. His attitude is nothing given, nothing gained; meaning, if you want a favor, you've got to pay for it somehow. You have to make an offering of respect. Offerings include bread, water, and treats for his dog, such as table scraps, dog food, and dog toys. When making prayer requests or after a prayer request is answered, he is offered figurines of dogs, rosaries, written thank-you notes, ceramic body parts, crosses, hearts, mementos, and thank-yous inscribed on bricks and photos.

The aspect of St. Roch that requires payment for services rendered is energized by left-handed magicians or sorcerers, whereby he is invoked for manipulative and harmful purposes. For example, just as people go to St. Roch for healing from physical disabilities, practitioners can petition him to target someone and *cause* physical disabilities.

When a petitioner is healed after praying to St. Roch, they will leave a crutch behind in the church since it is no longer needed. A left-handed conjure worker might craft an arm or leg out of clay, put it before St. Roch with the name of the target, and ask him to take that person's arm or leg. There's always a price for this kind of magick, however, as Nahnee, the Boss of Algiers and informant in Harry Middleton Hyatt's *Hoodoo-Witchcraft-Conjuration-Rootwork,* explains:

St. Roc will do favors, but he always takes somebody out de family. He's a vengeful saint. He'll do anything dat chew want done. If yo' want a individual to get a hand cut off, or to get a laig cut off or a finger—just how fur yo' want dat laig cut off tub dat person, up to de knee or all de way up to de hip, or if yo' want dey arm cut off up to de shoulder or somethin', or if yo' want dey haid mashed or anything of dat kind—yo' make somethin' of dat kind. You'll git clay, yo' see, an' you'll make an arm if it's an arm dat chew want cut off or if it's a laig, you'll make a foot . . . and you'll place dat before St. Roc . . . wit de name of dis individual dat chew want dis done to 'em, yo' see. If it's a white person, yo' write it on white papah an' red ink; an' if it's colored, yo' write it on brown papah wit black ink. An' yo' place dat foot or dat hand or whatsomevah yo' want wit dat name befo' dis picture of St. Roc. (Hyatt 1970–1978, vol. 1, 869)

Nahnee explains that the target's name should be written three times on the paper and placed under a yellow candle. The candle is to burn for nine days, which means the candle will be lit for a period of time each day, then extinguished, nine days in a row. Each time the candle is lit, the petitioner tells St. Roch what to do to the target, "an just like dat, dat's what will happen. Dat party will git in an accident or will git dat foot cut off" (Hyatt 1970–1978, vol. 2, 1374).

As has been noted, this type of magick is not without its consequences. Nahnee quickly pointed out that the typical price for a successful ritual is the death of someone you love more than life itself, a member of your family, usually the head of the household.

Nahnee wasn't the only conjure woman to report St. Roch's penchant for payment in flesh. A conjure woman named Ida Bates from New Orleans also reported something similar.

"St. Roch, he will do evil in this way," said Ida, "He will give flesh." She explains that you can make your petition to St. Roch for someone you desire and light your light to him and make your wish. You pay him what you promise to give him when he comes through. He gives you your desire, "but he'll take the one that you love dearer than what the Lord does. He give flesh, but he takes flesh . . . somebody will die" (Hyatt 1970–1978, vol. 2, 1654).

THE GHOSTS OF ST. ROCH CEMETERY

There are a number of ghosts associated with St. Roch's cemetery, including a dog and a hooded man. Ghosts in cemeteries in New Orleans are no surprise, given our cemeteries' reputation as the Cities of the Dead. Nor is it a surprise to find a ghost dog lurking about in the patron saint of dogs' final resting space.

There is nothing sinister about the ghost dog of St. Roch's cemetery. But then, I was born and raised in New Orleans and have been conducting séances since I was a little girl. That said, I assure you, the ghost dog is not scary. It is described as an unusually large black dog who simply meanders around the graveyard, seemingly keeping an eye on things. There have been no reports of it attacking anyone or facing down visitors, growling with teeth exposed. In fact, it typically moves in the opposite direction when spotted. Apparently, he looks so real that people have been known to follow it through the cemetery only to witness it vanish into thin air when it seems it has no other way of escaping.

The other most popular ghost in the cemetery is the man in the black cloak. Often referred to as the "Hooded Ghost," like the ghost dog, he is a benign spirit. He is seen walking throughout the cemetery at all hours of the day and night, wearing a long black robe with a hood pulled over his head. The thing that freaks people out about the Hooded Ghost is his ability to walk through the walls of the cemetery and even through tombs! When the cemetery gates are closed and it seems all have exited, he can be seen walking along the pathways. No one knows who this spirit is, but it is believed he was associated with the Church due to the period-specific garb he wears.

IN FINIS

St. Roch is an officially canonized saint by the Catholic Church yet is a folk saint in New Orleans in every sense of the phrase. As the special protector against plagues, epidemics, and pandemics, he is one of New Orleans's miracle workers. He is a saint we can turn to for healing, strength, and guidance in difficult times. He can help with love and legal issues and even assist with sorcery when energized as such. He even has something to give to those looking for a paranormal adventure.

Further, St. Roch Cemetery is a magickal cemetery where Doctor John is buried and where conjures of a special nature are performed. Since Doctor John is buried there, the two holy figures are connected spiritually. Both are renowned for their exceptional healing abilities, and both were of service to their respective communities.

Louis Martinie of the New Orleans Voodoo Spiritual Temple has referred to St. Roch as the guardian of Doctor John's bones. I think that descriptor is quite fitting. In short, St. Roch is surprisingly well rounded in his patronage and is an extremely helpful saint. One need only approach him with respect and humbly request his assistance, and he will answer.

20

Zozo LaBrique, Peddler of Red Brick Dust

"What was Zozo? Did she have any antecedents?" The old lady shrugged her shoulders and replied: "She has always been Zozo."

—LELONG'S GREAT-GRANDMOTHER

They say the reigning Voudou Queen of New Orleans pre-Marie Laveau was Sanité Dédé. Sanité Dede was a marchande, probably selling calas, a type of Creole pastry, in the local marketplace. At some point, she disappeared from the scene, and Zozo LaBrique took her place. But who was Zozo LaBrique?

Sadly, Zozo's story is a short one because we don't have much information about her. But her brick dust is legendary, and I believe that she simply must be better acknowledged. So, this story consists of what I could find out about the eccentric Queen from New Orleans, Zozo LaBrique, peddler of red brick dust.

Now she's neither a hoodoo saint nor a Voudou spirit, and all we have is local lore that says she was the reigning queen of the Voudous for a short time before Marie Laveau claimed her throne. Her reign as Voudou Queen was short-lived, however. Or maybe it didn't happen at all. I have been unable to locate any public documents or newspaper articles that support her connection to Voudou. Of course, that doesn't mean she wasn't a Voudou, only that I haven't found a way to prove or disprove it. One thing that remains true is that red brick dust being used for spiritual protection hasn't changed since Zozo peddled it by the bucketful in the 1800s.

In New Orleans, red bricks are used in pulverized dust form on the front steps of a home as a means of keeping evil away. Bricks were originally taken for ritual use from the Dumaine Street Brickyard—one of the earliest known places in New Orleans where Voudou rituals occurred. But the use of red brick dust in a spiritual context did not start in New Orleans or with Zozo LaBrique. There are descriptions about the medicinal use of red ochre clay in the Ebers Papyrus from Egypt, dating to about 1550 BCE (Ferguson 2006).

Cro-Magnon artists used red ochre pigments in prehistoric cave paintings in southern Europe between 32,000 and 10,000 years ago. Additionally, traditional African irosun powder is red dust produced by termites from the barwood (*Pterocarpus osun*) and camwood (*Baphia nitida*) trees and used in Ifá for divining purposes (Bascom 1991). The use of red brick dust could conceivably have found a place in the spiritual milieu of black American society due to its availability and the ingenuity of freed and enslaved Africans to adapt to their new environments.

Some people say we don't know Zozo's real name, but due to her appearance, she was called *zeauzeau,* meaning "bird" in Cajun French. *La brique* referenced the product she sold: crushed and pulverized red bricks. They say that children used to make fun of her because of how she looked. Nonetheless, she loved them and would affectionately caress their hair and give them peppermint sticks as treats. Apparently, Zozo only accepted payment for her brick dust in nickels, which she hoarded in her mattress.

Robert Tallant, the celebrated author from Louisiana, writes that Zozo LaBrique was actually Marie Saloppé, one of the Voudou Queens of New Orleans before Marie Laveau. According to him:

There are those who say Marie Saloppé became Zozo LaBrique, a well-known New Orleans street character, an apparently half-demented creature, who peddled buckets of brick dust. She was fixed, they say, by Marie Laveau because the latter wanted to rule the Voodoos alone. It has long been a custom among some New Orleans housewives to scrub their front steps with brick dust, a tradition having a definite connection with Voodoo—the washing away of an evil omen placed on the house by an enemy. It is true that now many people will tell you that they do this only for reasons of cleanliness; yet that was its original meaning, and many stoops in the poorer section of the city have a well-scrubbed, whitish appearance, showing that brick dust has been used. Zozo LaBrique sold her dust for a nickel a bucket, and when she died, a small fortune in those coins is said to have been found in her disreputable quarters. (Tallant 1984, 47)

When I reviewed the same field notes that Tallant had used for his writing, there was no mention of Zozo LaBrique being Marie Saloppé. On the contrary, her name was Menard, as reported by her neighbor, who seemed to be a credible witness. It may be that Zozo's relationship to Marie Saloppé is a case of Tallant's flair for embellishment; a storytelling style so convincing it has been the go-to source for facts about New Orleans Voudou for everyone and their mother's brother for forever and a day now.

Arguably, Zozo's story does lend itself to embellishment since we have little else to go on. I did find a 1940 reference to her by a French man named Lelong in notes by the Federal Writers' Project (FWP). Lelong knew Zozo LaBrique and said he purchased brick dust by the bucketful from her for one nickel. He shared some memories of her:

I can still visualize the woman shouldering her way through the changing back gates, tall, thin, and erect with a filled bucket on her matted grey head carrying in each hand another one. Her eyes, flashing over her hawk's nose, mumbling, she would talk to the kitchen door and screech "La brique pilée!" (meaning *crushed brick*). Upon receiving her pay and a cup of coffee, she would dump the contents into its proper receptacle and, without a word, leave the place. Other times I have seen her dragging a box full of soft bricks she had culled from some dilapidated building—where she lived no one seems to know. (Lelong 1940)

Sidewalks in New Orleans prior to 1895 were made from flagstones or red bricks. Lelong described how his own sidewalk, garden walk, backyard, and kitchen floor were made of bricks. The bricks were scrubbed each morning with a solution of brick dust and water, as was customary, to prevent grass from growing between the cracks. At least that's how the white folks did it. Now the black folks, they mixed that dust with urine due to the belief that the combination is ideal for spiritual protection.

Lelong remembered Zozo from when he was a child and recalled, "As a child, I sensed that the negroes of the house held her in awesome regard and seemed anxious not to anger her. I never asked the reason." She was always dressed in "faded grey calico, bare-legged and wearing the same pair of cast-off men's shoes," and she always appeared busy on her way to sell her wares or gather raw material from which to make her magick dust. To him, she seemed to be ageless, "something that the elements had shaped into the likeness of a human being," with the brick dust permeating every pore of her body. Despite how poor she seemed to be, she never begged for anything.

On his way home from school one day, Lelong inquired about Zozo. Sadly, he learned she had died from malnutrition. In a stunning revelation, thousands of dollars belonging to her were found in her mattress following her death!

Perhaps the best description we have of Zozo LaBrique comes from a black woman named Anita Fonvergne, who was interviewed by the Federal Writers' Project in 1939. According to Anita, Zozo was her neighbor. They lived right across the street from each other:

Zozo LaBrique used to live right across from us . . . she had brown hair and blue eyes and was fair. She used to get the bricks and pound them and make her dust, and then she'd carry it in two pails and a pail on her head. Her name was Menard, and she's related to some of the nicest families here. Zozo means bird, and that's just a nickname they gave her. She was good to us, we were children then, and in the evening, she would buy peppermint sticks and give us all a piece. She wouldn't bother anybody, and she never talked to anybody much. . . .

We used to tease her a lot, and whenever we'd see a bird, we'd tell her in French, "Zozo, look at the bird," and the only thing she would say is "tsh" and turn her head. She never cursed anybody or sassed them; she just minded her business. (Breaux 1939, Folder 541, 8)

Today, Zozo LaBrique is as much a mystery as she was back in the 1800s. When Lelong asked his great-grandmother, who was in her nineties at the time, "What was Zozo? Did she have any antecedents?" The old lady shrugged her shoulders and replied: "She has always been Zozo" (Lelong 1940, 14).

References

Aldrich, Thomas Bailey. 1873. *Père Antoine's Date-Palm*. Boston and New York: Houghton Mifflin Company.

Alvarado, Denise. 2013. *The Conjurer's Guide to St. Expedite*. Prescott Valley, AZ: Creole Moon Publications.

———. 2017. *Denise M. Alvarado's Anthology of Conjure*. Prescott Valley, AZ: Creole Moon Publications.

———. 2020. *The Magic of Marie Laveau: Embracing the Spiritual Legacy of the Voodoo Queen of New Orleans*. Weiser Books: San Francisco.

Asbury, Herbert. 1936. *French Quarter: An Informal History of New Orleans' Underworld*. New York: Thunder's Mouth Press.

Bascom, William W. 1991. *Ifa Divination: Communication between Gods and Men in West Africa*. Bloomington: Indiana University Press.

Baton Rouge (LA) Gazette. 1844. "Witchcraft and Superstition." June 15, 1844.

Berry, Jason. 1995. *The Spirit of Black Hawk: A Mystery of Africans and Indians*. Jackson, Mississippi: University Press of Mississippi.

———. 1998. "The Cult of Black Hawk." *Chicago Tribune*. www.chicagotribune.com

Black Hawk. (1833) 1882. *Autobiography of 'Ma-Ka-Tai-Me-She-Kia-Kiak' or Black Hawk*. Edited by J. B. Patterson. St. Louis: Continental Printing.

Blier, Suzanne Preston. 1996. *African Vodun: Art, Psychology, and Power*. Chicago: University of Chicago Press.

Bolton, Herbert Eugene, and Thomas Maitland Marshall. 1920. *The Colonization of North America, 1492–1783*. New York: The Macmillan Company.

Bookhardt, Eric D. 1986. "That Voodoo That We Do." *Wavelength*. September, 26–27. *scholarworks.uno.edu*

Breaux, Hazel. 1939. Folder 541. "Life History." In *Voodoo, 1937–1941*, edited by Catherine Dillon. Unpublished manuscript. Louisiana Writers' Project (LWP), Federal Writers' Collection. Watson Memorial Library, Cammie G. Henry Research Center, Northwestern State University, Natchitoches, Louisiana.

Brown, Nicholas A., and Sara E. Kanouse. 2015. *Recollecting Black Hawk*. Pittsburgh: University of Pittsburgh Press.

Calgary (Alberta) Herald. 1977. "People." July 13, 1977, 15.

Castellanos, Henry. 1895. *New Orleans as It Was: Episodes of Louisiana Life.* New Orleans: L. Graham & Son.

Chery, Dady. 2012. "Akasan, Haitian Cornmeal Drink for Sunday Morning." *www.dadychery.org*

Cincinnati Inquirer. 1911. "Daily Divorce Doings." January 29, 1911, 7, 17.

Cleary, G. 1912. "St. Roch." In *The Catholic Encyclopedia*. New York: Robert Appleton Company. Retrieved September 8, 2014, from New Advent: *www.newadvent.org*

Conrad, William. 1956. "The Legend of Annie Christmas." The CBS Radio Workshop, episode no. 38. CBS, October 19.

Crowley (LA) Post-Signal. 1977. "'Head' Mystery Solved." July 13, 1977, 2.

Dadswell, Jack. 1946. "Jack Visits Tomb of Voodoo Priestess." *Tampa Bay Times* (St. Petersburg, FL). December 10, 1946, 16.

Daily Republican (Wilmington, DE). 1879. "Dr. Peebles, the Lecturer." December 15, 1879, 3.

Daily World (Opelousas, LA). 1972. "High Priestess of Louisiana's Witches Ready for Ceremonies." October 31, 1972, 3.

Davis, Erik. 1991. "Trickster at the Crossroads: West Africa's God of Messages, Sex, and Deceit." *Gnosis* 14, no. 26. (Copy available at *www.mamiwata.com,* accessed September 2, 2020.)

Dillon, Catherine. Folders 025, 029, 043, 044, 550, and 575. *Voodoo, 1937–1941.* Unpublished manuscript. Louisiana Writers' Project (LWP), Federal Writers' Collection. Watson Memorial Library, Cammie G. Henry Research Center, Northwestern State University, Natchitoches, Louisiana.

Ellis, Albert B. 1965. *The Ewe Speaking Peoples of the Slave Coast of West Africa.* Chicago: Benin Press.

Evening Republican (Meadville, PA). 1915. "Nineteen Known Dead Result of Great Storm." October 1, 1915, 4.

Fensterstock, Alison. 2018. "The High Priestess of the French Quarter." *64 Parishes. 64parishes.org*

Ferguson, J. B. 2006. "The Ebers Papyrus Possibly Having to Do with Diabetes Mellitus." Annandale-on-Hudson, New York: Bard College.

Fowler Museum, The. 2012. "In Extremis: Death and Life in 21st-Century Haitian Art." Los Angeles: Fowler Museum of Cultural History.

France, Renée Souladre-La. "Slaves, Saints and Statues: Baroque Catholic Imagery and African Sensibilities from Nueva Granada." *Revista Canadiense De Estudios Hispánicos* 33, no. 1 (2008): 215–229. Accessed February 18, 2020. *www.jstor.org*

Gandolfo, Charles. 1992. *Marie Laveau of New Orleans.* New Orleans: New Orleans Historic Voodoo Museum.

Gaudet, Marcia, and James McDonald. 2003. *Mardi Gras, Gumbo, and Zydeco: Readings in Louisiana Culture.* Jackson, Mississippi: University Press of Mississippi.

Gaul, Alma. 2015. "Researcher Questions What Happened to Black Hawk's Bones." *Quad-City Times* (Davenport, Iowa), October 26, 2015. Updated February 18, 2020.

Gemfyre. n.d. "Frenier Cemetery." Atlas Obscura. *www.atlasobscura.com*

Gray, D. R. 2015. "A Manger in a Sea of Mud: Material Legacies and Loss at the Temple of the Innocent Blood." *Archeological Papers of the American Anthropological Association* 26: 105–121. doi:10.1111/apaa.12062.

Guillory, Margarita Simon. 2011. "Creating Selves: An Interdisciplinary Exploration of Self and Creativity in African American Religion." Dissertation, 2011. *core.ac.uk*

Hall, Gwendolyn Midlo. 1992. *Africans in Colonial Louisiana: The Development of Afro-Creole Culture in the Eighteenth Century.* Baton Rouge: Louisiana State University Press.

Haskin, Jim. 1961. "Annie Christmas Known as Female Bunyan in South." *The Times* (Munster, Indiana), December 17, 1961.

Hattiesburg (MI) American. 1978. "Halloween is No Joke to New Orleans Witch." October 31, 1978.

Hearn, Lafcadio. 1924. "The Last of the Voudous." In *An American Miscellany 2*, edited by Albert Mordell. New York: Dodd, Mead and Company.

Hurston, Zora Neale. 1943. "High John de Conquer." *American Mercury* 57. October 1943, 452.

Hyatt, Harry Middleton. 1970–1978. *Hoodoo-Conjuration-Witchcraft-Rootwork,* vols. 1–5. Cambridge, MD: Western Publishing Co.

Indianapolis (IN) News. 1915. "Storm Death List in the South Grows." October 1, 1915, 10.

Kolb, Carolyn. 2013. *New Orleans Memories: One Writer's City.* Jackson, Miss.: University of Mississippi Press.

Langford, Nathaniel Pitt. 1901. "The Louisiana Purchase and Preceding Spanish Intrigues for Dismemberment of the Union." St. Paul, Minn.: Minnesota Historical Society.

Leggett, Richard C. 1944. "An Historic Indian Agency." *The Annals of Iowa* 25. 257–274.

Lelong, P. A. 1940. Folder 550. "Zozo la Brique." In *Voodoo, 1937–1941*, edited by Catherine Dillon. Unpublished manuscript. Louisiana Writers' Project (LWP), Federal Writers' Collection. Watson Memorial Library, Cammie G. Henry Research Center, Northwestern State University, Natchitoches, Louisiana.

Long, Carolyn Morrow. 1997. "John the Conqueror: From Root-Charm to Commercial Product." *Pharmacy in History* 39, no. 2: 47–53. Accessed September 30, 2020. *www.jstor.org*

Los Angeles Times. 1926. "New Orleans Shrine Popular with Girls." March 10, 1926, 4.

Martinic, Louis. 2014. *Dr. John Montanee: A Grimoire*. New Orleans: Black Moon Publishing.

McKinney, Robert. Folder 210. "Saint Black Hawk—Indian Worshipped by Spiritualists." In *Voodoo, 1937–1941*, edited by Catherine Dillon. Unpublished manuscript. Louisiana Writers' Project (LWP), Federal Writers' Collection. Watson Memorial Library, Cammie G. Henry Research Center, Northwestern State University, Natchitoches, Louisiana.

———. 1937. Folder 043. "St. Peter and Black Cat Opening." In *Voodoo, 1937–1941*, edited by Catherine Dillon. Unpublished manuscript. Louisiana Writers' Project (LWP), Federal Writers' Collection. Watson Memorial Library, Cammie G. Henry Research Center, Northwestern State University, Natchitoches, Louisiana.

Métraux, Alfred. (1959) 1972. *Voodoo in Haiti*. Trans. Hugo Charteris. New York: Schocken Books.

Michinard. 1941. "Interview with Ex-Slave Josephine McDuffy in 1941." State Library of Louisiana/Louisiana Works Progress Administration. Accessed July 29, 2020. *louisianadigitallibrary.org*

Miller, Bobbi. 2013. *Big River's Daughter*. New York, NY: Holiday House.

Miracles of the Saints. 2010. "S.A.G. St. Anthony Guide—Miraculous Letter
    Deliveries." Accessed July 20, 2020. *www.miraclesofthesaints.com*

New Orleans Crescent. 1850. "The Rites of Voudou." July 31, 1850.

New Orleans Official Tourism Bureau. 2012. "New Orleans Sports Teams:
    New Orleans VooDoo Arena Football." *www.neworleansonline.com*

New Orleans Weekly Delta. 1850. "Voudouism Unveiled." August 5, 1850.

New York Times. 1896. "Long Island." September 17, 1896.

Oakland (CA) Tribune. 1926. "Doctor John." February 7, 1926, 74.

O'Brien, M. S. 2004. "Saint Expedtitus Don't Get No Respect." Aliens in
    this World website. *suburbanbanshee.wordpress.com*

Onofrio, Jan. 1999. *Louisiana Biographical Dictionary.* St. Clair Shores,
    Michigan: Somerset Publishers.

Paul, John, Krystal Luce, and Sharla Blank. 2013. "'Playing Vodou': A Visual
    Essay of Imitation and Meaning in Political and Popular Cultural
    Depictions of Baron Samedi." *International Journal of Humanities
    and Social Science* 3, no. 6 (0AD): 287–301.

Pedersen, Nicole Biguenet. 2011. "NOLA History: The Night the Inquisi-
    tion Came to Town." GoNola, September 21. Accessed January
    24, 2019. *gonola.com*

Pitkin, Helen. 1904. *An Angel by Brevet.* Philadelphia: J. B. Lippincott
    Company.

Pittsburgh Courier. 1927. "Pay Last Respects to Mother Anderson." Decem-
    ber 24, 1927, 8.

Posey, Zoe. 1939. "Quest for Marie Laveau's Burial Place in New Orleans
    Louisiana." State Library of Louisiana/Louisiana Works Progress
    Administration.

Pustanio, Alyne. 2013. "The Story of Mary Oneida Toups." In *Hoodoo and
    Conjure New Orleans,* edited by Denise Alvarado. Prescott Valley,
    AZ: Creole Moon Publications, 64–71.

Rebennack, Mac, and Jack Rummel. 1994. *Under a Hoodoo Moon*. New York: St. Martin's Press.

Sanfield, Steve, and John Ward. 1995. *The Adventures of High John the Conqueror*. Little Rock, AR: August House.

Saxon, Lyle. 1927. *Father Mississippi*. Gretna, La.: Pelican Publishing Company.

———. 1928. *Fabulous New Orleans*. Gretna, La.: Pelican Publishing Company.

———. 1945. *Gumbo Ya-Ya: A Collection of Louisiana Folk Tales*. Boston: MA: Houghton Mifflin Company.

Scott, Mike. 2017. "Who Was Père Antoine? And Why Is an Alley Named after Him?" *Times-Picayune* online at *Nola.com*. April 23, 2017; updated July 7, 2021. *www.nola.com*

Simpson, George Eaton. 1945. "The Belief System of Haitian Vodun." *American Anthropologist* 47, no. 1: 35–59. doi:10.1525/aa.1945.47.1.02a00030.

Snyder, J. F. 1911. "The Burial and Resurrection of Black Hawk." *Journal of the Illinois State Historical Society (1908-1984)* 4, no. 1: 47–56. Accessed September 9, 2019. *www.jstor.org*

Sobol, Louis. 1939. "The New Cavalcade." *Herald and Examiner* (New York). March 1, 1939.

Spraker, Eileen C. 1973. "Witch Priestess Takes Religion Seriously." *Morning News* (Wilmington, Delaware). July 28, 1973, 16.

St. Louis Cathedral. n.d. "The Year of Calamity." From "Our History." *www.stlouiscathedral.org*

Sunday Delta, The (New Orleans, Louisiana). 1860. "A Voudouest Disgorged." October 21, 1860, 8.

Sutton, Horace. 1972. "Mumbo Jumbo Prevails in New Orleans." *Baltimore Sun* (Baltimore, Maryland). August 20.

Swetnam, George. 1968. "She Bluffed Mike Fink?" *The Pittsburgh Press* (Pittsburgh, Pennsylvania). April 14, 135.

Tallant, Robert. 1946. *Voodoo in New Orleans*. New Orleans: Pelican.

———. 1984. *The Voodoo Queen*. New Orleans: Arcadia Publishing.

Thomas, James W. 2011. "Roark Bradford." In *Encyclopedia of Louisiana*, edited by David Johnson. Louisiana Endowment for the Humanities, 2010–. Article published May 23. *64parishes.org*

Thompson, John. 1948. "Annie Christmas." *The Tennessean*. October 24.

Thornton, John K. 1988. "On the Trail of Voodoo: African Christianity in African and the Americas." *Americas* 44, no. 3: 268–71.

Times (Munster, IN). 1938. "Two New Orleans Shrines Visited by Sufferers for Generations Leave Many Odd Offerings." March 24, 1938, 11.

Times Daily Picayune (New Orleans, LA). 1890. "Voudouism." June 22, 1890, 10.

Times-Democrat (New Orleans, LA). 1875. "Under the Spell." October 27, 1875, 3.

Times-Picayune (New Orleans, LA). n.d. "1915 Hurricane." Retrieved from microfilm by Gladys Stovall Armstrong. *usgwarchives.net*

———. 1844. "The Days of Witchcraft Returning." June 7, 1844, 2.

———. 1850. "More of the Voudous." July 31, 1850, 1–2.

———. 1874. "The Courts: Fourth District Court." February 21, 1874, 2.

———. 1885. "Our Picayunes." March 8, 1885.

Trevigne, Barbara. 2010. "Ball of Confusion." *New Orleans Genesis* 48, no. 192 (October): 319–23.

Wallace, Maude. 1940. Folder 237. "Lala." In *Voodoo, 1937–1941*, edited by Catherine Dillon. Unpublished manuscript. Louisiana Writers' Project (LWP), Federal Writers' Collection. Watson Memorial Library, Cammie G. Henry Research Center, Northwestern State University, Natchitoches, Louisiana.

Wichita (KS) Beacon. 1915. "Water Subsides in New Orleans." September 30, 1915, 12.

Williams, Claudia. 2020. "Dr John Altar." Email communication, October 11.

Williams, Karen. 2011. "St Expedito's Role in South Louisiana Catholicism, in New Orleans and in the Italian-American Community Near Independence, Louisiana." *Louisiana Folklore Miscellany* 65.

ADDITIONAL READING

Alvarado, Denise. "Annie Christmas: A New Orleans Voudou Loa." The Voodoo Muse. *www.voodoomuse.org*

———. *The Voodoo Hoodoo Spellbook*. Weiser Books: San Francisco, 2011.

Barnes, Bruce "Sunpie," and Rachel Breunlin. "Pasajs/Passages for San Malo." South Writ Large, 2019. *southwritlarge.com*

Bradford, Mary Rose. "The Story of Annie Christmas," in *A Treasury of Mississippi River Folklore*, edited by B. A. Botkin, 35. New York: Crown, 1955.

Butler, Alban. *The Lives of the Fathers, Martyrs, and Other Principal Saints.* Dublin: James Duffy, 1866; Bartleby.com, 2010. *www.bartleby.com/210.*

Cable, George W. "Creole Slave Songs." *Century Illustrated Monthly Magazine* 31, no. 6 (April 1886): 807–828.

Charleston (SC) Daily News. "Congo Court Gossip." June 17, 1869.

Cincinnati Enquirer. "The Voudoux and Their Charms." May 29, 1868.

———. "News of the Courts." December 23, 1911.

de Caro, Frank. "Legends, Local Identity, and a New Orleans Cookbook." *Louisiana Folklore Miscellany* 9 (2009): 23–31.

Din, Gilbert C. "'Cimarrones' and the San Malo Band in Spanish Louisiana." *Louisiana History: The Journal of the Louisiana Historical Association* 21, no. 3 (1980): 237–62.

Diouf, Sylviane A. *Slavery's Exiles: The Story of the American Maroons.* New York: NYU Press, 2014.

Douglas, Nick. "Know Your Black History: Juan St. Malo." *Afro Punk* (June 17, 2014). *afropunk.com*

Frost, Meigs O. "Annie Christmas," *NOTP Magazine* (23 May 1948): 16.

Green, Laura Marcus. "St. Joseph's Altars: Faith in Tradition." Folklife in Louisiana, 2016. *www.louisianafolklife.org*

Hamilton, Virginia. *Her Stories: African American Folktales, Fairy Tales, and True Tales.* New York: Scholastic Inc., 1995.

Hearn, Lafcadio. "St. Malo: A Lacustrine Village in Louisiana." *Harper's Weekly Magazine* (March 31, 1883).

Herskovits, Melville J. "African Gods and Catholic Saints in New World Negro Belief." *American Anthropologist* 39, no. 4 (1937): 635–43. doi:10.1525/aa.1937.39.4.02a00080.

Hunter, David. "New Orleans: Dining At All Hours." *Cincinnati Inquirer.* September 5, 1971, 42.

Kaplan-Levenson, Laine. "More Than a Runaway: Maroons in Louisiana." KEDM Public Radio. December 10, 2015. *www.kedm.org*

Kirsch, Johann Peter. "St. Peter, Prince of the Apostles." In *The Catholic Encyclopedia,* vol. 11. New York: Robert Appleton Company, 1911. Retrieved October 25, 2020, from New Advent. *www.newadvent.org.*

Kosloski, Philip. "How to Venerate a Saint's Relic." Aleteia. May 26, 2017. *aleteia.org*

Lovejoy, Bess. "The Legend (and Truth) of the Voodoo Priestess Who Haunts a Louisiana Swamp." Mentalfloss. October 14, 2017. *mentalfloss.com*

Mershman, Francis. "St. Raymond Nonnatus." In *The Catholic Encyclopedia,* vol. 12. New York: Robert Appleton Company, 1911. Retrieved August 2, 2020, from New Advent. *www.newadvent.org*

New Orleans Republican. "Extreme Penalty of the Law, Death Punishment for Murder." May 14, 1871.

Newland, Mary Reed. *The Year and Our Children.* New York: P. J. Kenedy & Sons, 1956.

O'Toole, Thomas J. "Sure, but Can She Turn Us into Rabbits?" *Daily News* (October 27, 1974).

Saunders, William. "Church Teaching on Relics." *Arlington Catholic Herald* (2003), from Catholic Education Resource Center. *www.catholiceducation.org*

Swancer, Brent. "Voodoo, Ghosts, and Werewolves at Louisiana's Cursed Swamp." Mysterious Universe. January 6, 2016. *mysteriousuniverse.org*

Thomas, James W. *Lyle Saxon: A Critical Biography.* Birmingham, Alabama: Summa Publications, Inc., 1991.

Whitfield, Mallory. "GoNOLA Find: Popp's Fountain in City Park." GoNOLA. July 5, 2014. *gonola.com*

THE AUTHOR'S ONLINE RESOURCES

The following are among a network of educational resources that I provide for the accurate dispersion of cultural information related to Southern folkways, folk magick, and folk life.

American Rootwork Association

www.americanrooworkassociation.com

The American Rootwork Association (ARA) is an evolving coalition of practicing rootworkers, scholars, scholar-practitioners, and tradition-keepers interested in formalizing the study of rootwork, rootdoctoring, and related folk traditions as serious areas of scientific and cultural inquiry.

Conjure Club

www.conjurecub.com

Creole Moon's Conjure Club is the ideal solution for anyone who is concerned about continuing their conjure education on a regular basis. Our eBooks and downloads give you alternative points of view and a variety of perspectives to enhance understanding of the conjure arts and to enrich and improve conjuring skills.

Conjure Doctors and Spiritual Mothers

www.conjuredoctors.com

This website is devoted to honoring the ancestors of the hoodoo, conjure, and rootwork traditions. It provides free information about conjure doctor cures, remedies, core practices, harms and cures, household receipts, articles, resources, and an alternate perspective on the history of hoodoo.

Creole Moon Publications and Spiritual Supplies

www.creolemoon.com

This is my primary website for self-published books and magazines, plus a variety of spiritual supplies that inspire, guide, and enrich daily living. From artistic devotional candles, aromatherapy oils, and perfumes to aromatic bath salts and a few good books to read, every product is designed to promote a lifestyle filled with magick.

Crossroads University

www.crossroadsuniversity.com

Crossroads University is an innovative cultural learning program that is dedicated to the observation and preservation of the folk magick traditions of the American South.

Marie-Laveaux

www.marie-laveaux.com

The exclusive website based on the book, *The Magic of Marie Laveaux*. Find excerpts, articles, recipes, and more about the life of the Voodoo Queen of New Orleans.

Denise Alvarado on Patreon

www.patreon.com/denisealvarado

Support me by joining Patreon and receive exclusive previews of my new and upcoming books, zines, art, and blog posts.

About the Author

DENISE ALVARADO was born and raised in the rich Creole culture of New Orleans and has studied indigenous healing traditions for over four decades. She is a rootworker in the Louisiana folk magic tradition, a spiritual artist, and a teacher of Southern conjure at Crossroads University. The author of numerous books about Southern folk traditions, including the *The Conjurer's Guide to St. Expedite*, *The Voodoo Hoodoo Spellbook*, *The Magic of Marie Laveau*, and *The Voodoo Doll Spellbook*, her artwork has been featured on several television shows. Visit her at *creolemoon.com*.

Find her on Social Media

Instagram: *@creole_moon and @authorDeniseAlvarado*

Pinterest: *www.pinterest.com/voodoomama*

Tumblr: *neworleansvoudou.tumblr.com*

Facebook: *facebook.com/AuthorDeniseAlvarado*

Twitter: *@voodoomuse1 and @VoodooMamaOG*

To Our Readers

Weiser Books, an imprint of Red Wheel/Weiser, publishes books across the entire spectrum of occult, esoteric, speculative, and New Age subjects. Our mission is to publish quality books that will make a difference in people's lives without advocating any one particular path or field of study. We value the integrity, originality, and depth of knowledge of our authors.

Our readers are our most important resource, and we appreciate your input, suggestions, and ideas about what you would like to see published.

Visit our website at *www.redwheelweiser.com*, where you can learn about our upcoming books and free downloads, and also find links to sign up for our newsletter and exclusive offers.

You can also contact us at *info@rwwbooks.com* or at

Red Wheel/Weiser, LLC

65 Parker Street, Suite 7

Newburyport, MA 01950

PV 4/2022